Praise for *Tam*

No fluff, straight to the point and packed to the brim with brilliant advice, there is no book quite like *Tame Your Tiger* for getting right to the heart of the issues faced by small product business owners today. If you sell products, you need to read this!

Michelle Ovens CBE, Founder,
Small Business Britain

In this book Catherine takes her years of experience of working for big retailers in the UK and overseas to distill good practice for the benefit of small businesses. If you are a product-based business wanting to work smarter not harder in achieving results and get on top of your finances, this is a must-read!

Emma Jones CBE, Founder, Enterprise Nation

As a small business owner, the right support and good advice can often be hard to find; enter *Tame Your Tiger: How to stop your product business eating you alive*. Filled with practical tips and advice, this is an absolute must-have for every business owner!

Louise Daniel, Founder, And so to Shop

Catherine's book is a brilliant resource for independent retail businesses – it's fantastic to have something that is so directly relevant to this sector. The tiger analogy works brilliantly and makes a complex area easier to understand – we will definitely be recommending this book as a top resource for Crafty Fox's artists and makers.

Sinead Koehler, Founder and Director,
Crafty Fox Market

Catherine's managed to make complex and scary subjects including margin, profit and stock planning, easy to understand for even the most creative of us (myself included).

I can't think of many brands that I've worked with over the past decade that wouldn't benefit from reading this book. Your business will be so much easier to run after doing so.

Rosie Davies-Smith, Founder, PR Dispatch

A highly practical resource to help product-based brands get a firm grip on their finances, margins, pricing and growth opportunities. Chock-full of detail, useful information, calculations and how-to guides to help you understand the numbers behind your business so you can make better, more profitable decisions and ensure the resilience and longevity of your brand.

JUST A CARD campaign team

A must-read for the owner of any small or medium-sized business! Catherine successfully breaks down how to calculate and understand important metrics in simple, practical and engaging exercises. A wealth of knowledge and actionable tips, a brilliant book I feel every business owner can learn from. I wish this was available when I was starting out!

Chloe Torpey, Founder, Olive and Frank

Catherine knows her numbers, and if you own a business selling products then so should you! This book is packed with tips for how to manage the money in your business. Ignore her advice at your peril.

Kate Hills, Founder and CEO, Make It British

Catherine is certainly attuned to the environment that she works in and has her finger on the pulse for the benefit of the industry. This book is essential for anyone who is in business, both new or seasoned, as there is some fantastic advice, goals and ideas to help your business succeed, all in a refreshing new approach.

Chris Workman, Marketing and PR Manager,
The Giftware Association

This book's power lies in taking complex subjects and making them accessible to small business owners. Whether you think of yourself as a numbers person or not, *Tame Your Tiger* will help you get clear on the key figures to keep an eye on to help you feel in control of your product business. Highly recommended.

Rachel Westall, Editor, *Craft Focus*

An essential book for any stage of your retail business journey! A must-read to ensure you know your figures and maximize profitability. With useful case studies, tips and tricks, it will help you to visualize and apply the content. Definitely one for your business toolbox!

Nicki Capewell, Founder, Pedddle

Catherine takes an honest and down-to-earth approach to navigating the minefield that is growing your product business. Calm, warm and hugely relatable, she successfully breaks down a product business into digestible pieces of practical advice, from understanding your finances to selling successfully online. This book will help product-based business owners make sense of a fast-moving market.

Dirk Bischof, Chief Executive of Hatch Enterprise

An essential read for any product business owner or founder who wants to get off the roller coaster and into the driving seat. Packed with insightful tips and industry know-how, this is the book you need to ensure your business is built on strong foundations.

Helen Carley, Entrepreneurship Advice Manager,
University of Brighton

Tame Your Tiger is a fantastic resource for retailers looking to wrestle back control of their business. Catherine simplifies key business metrics and gives practical, digestible advice. She gets straight to the point and the end result is a really valuable business book.

Rob Gamage, Managing Editor, *Modern Retail*

How to stop your
product business
eating you alive

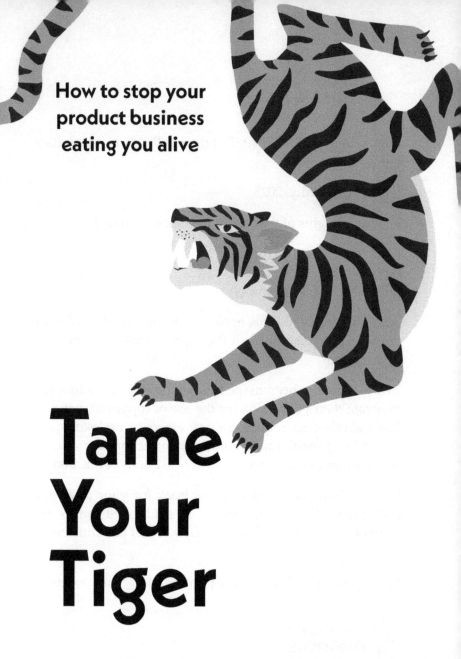

Tame
Your
Tiger

CATHERINE ERDLY

First published in Great Britain by Practical Inspiration Publishing, 2023

© Catherine Erdly, 2023

The moral rights of the author have been asserted

ISBN 9781788604048 (print)
ISBN 9781788604062 (epub)
ISBN 9781788604055 (mobi)

Want to bulk-buy copies of this book for your team and colleagues? We can introduce case studies, customize the content and co-brand *Tame Your Tiger* to suit your business's needs.

Please email info@practicalinspiration.com for more details.

This book is dedicated to all the resilient retailers, especially my club members and clients, who never cease to inspire me with their creativity and determination.

CONTENTS

CHAPTER 1

DO YOU HAVE A TIGER IN YOUR BUSINESS?

Do you want to know how to improve your relationship with your product business?

Many people start product businesses because they love creating or curating beautiful products. However, they often find themselves on a steep learning curve, grappling with how to actually make money.

Imagine this. One day you see an adorable stripy ball of fur and can't resist taking it home. You feed it, love it, constantly think of ways to improve its life and care for it. Then one day, after you find yourself yet again trying to figure out what this creature wants, you realize that instead of a tame tabby cat, you are actually the owner of a fully grown tiger.

Product businesses are like that. They seem incredibly appealing when you are first starting out; then, before you know it, you are at the deep end trying to figure out what on earth to do.

How do you know if you have a tiger in your business? The easiest way to understand this is to think about how your business makes you feel.

Do any of the following sound familiar?

- You feel constantly on the back foot and your business seems unpredictable.
- You wonder if you are out of your depth.
- There doesn't seem to be enough money to get the help you need, so as you grow and get busier, you seem to be doing more and more instead of being able to step away.
- The business seems to be demanding increasing amounts of money so as soon as you have sales coming in, money is going straight out again to cover stock or other expenses.

If your business makes you nervous, feels unpredictable or seems to have turned into a hungry cash-consuming monster, then you have a tiger business.

Who is this book for?

If any of the above sounds familiar, do not worry! This book exists solely to help you feel more confident and in control of your business. It will be relevant whether you've run your business for several years or are just starting out.

The book is also applicable to different models of product businesses, whether you have a bricks and mortar shop, an e-commerce store or a mixture of both.

The principles will be relevant whether you make the products you sell or curate them from other businesses. The same applies whether you sell through your own website, someone else's website or directly to the public. Ultimately, if you sell products to people, this book is for you.

A note on the word "retail"

When I use the word "retail", people often assume that I am either speaking about large retailers or referring specifically to bricks and mortar stores.

Dictionary.com has the following definition of the word: "the sale of goods to ultimate consumers, usually in small quantities (opposed to wholesale)". In other words, selling things to people.

This definition does not distinguish between selling online or offline, which is something I wholeheartedly agree with. When I use the term "retail" I am not just referring to bricks and mortar stores, but to everyone who sells products.

Why I wrote this book

I wrote this book in direct response to all the people who have said things to me like "I grew my sales last year but somehow did not break even" or "I don't understand how I can be making sales but I'm always running out of cash".

It's designed to help you answer these kinds of questions and ultimately change the way you feel about your business.

Before reading this book

You feel unsure of yourself or frustrated with your inability to manage your business. A common phenomenon is something I call "the hot flush of shame". It's that feeling you get when you think you should know certain numbers or facts about your business. But you never take the time to look because you don't know where to start or even why these numbers are important.

You feel lost or overwhelmed, wondering if you will ever work out how to make money. Some successes come your way but even as your sales grow, you feel stuck and unsure about how or why these sales successes are not translating into profitability, or why your profitability is lower than before.

Without a solid understanding of what numbers you should be aiming for, you can feel a little bit lost. What's more, even if you do set yourself goals, you don't know what actions to take if you are not hitting or exceeding your goals.

After reading this book

Once you have used the tools and exercises in this book to examine your business, you'll have a clear understanding of your strengths and areas of development. You'll be able to explore what is impacting your profitability and what you can do about it.

Moreover, you'll have a plan to navigate the ups and the downs of retail sales. Product businesses are constantly changing. It's what makes them fun and exciting, but also challenging.

The purpose behind the ideas in the book is to help you create a framework and a basis for understanding how your business makes money.

Helping you see:

- which products make you the most profit;
- where you should be focusing your time;

- what you can afford in terms of expenses;
- how much stock you should have;
- what to do if you've got too much stock;
- what to do if sales are tough.

Over time, these learnings will allow you to assess how well things are working.

The fundamentals of making money in retail

This whole book is dedicated to the fundamental, never-changing ways to make profit in a retail business. Sales tactics or marketing trends come and go, but this book tackles the underlying principles that always govern how product businesses make money.

These principles won't change as your business grows. I've used them to manage budgets of up to £400 million and we were looking at exactly the same metrics that are in this book.

But if any of your business fundamentals are weak, then your business will only become more difficult to manage as it grows. Working through this book will help you build a firm foundation that will take you far.

What does the book require from you?

To get the most out of this book, you need an open mind. You may not consider yourself as a numbers person, or perhaps you do. You also may firmly believe that you did not start your product business to spend time number crunching.

However, honing in on these numbers helps you stay focused. I will only ever ask you to calculate a number, check a statistic or look at data if it is going to help you in some way make better decisions about your business.

It also requires you to work through the "hot flush of shame". If at any point you feel stressed or anxious about why you don't already know some of these numbers, then I simply ask you to be kind to yourself.

Much of what we're covering comes from my experience in the retail industry (more on this later), so unless you also have a background in driving profits in retailers, it's not surprising that you don't know what you don't know.

What does it not require?

The book requires a willingness to engage with the numbers in your business, but most of the calculations used are simple.

You will not need any specific type of software or expensive tools to run your calculations. All the spreadsheets described in the book can be created in Google Sheets, which is a free spreadsheet software.

There are also lots of additional bonus materials to support you as you work through the book – check the 'Additional resources' section at the end for more details.

How to use this book

Ultimately, how you use this book is up to you, but it is designed to be read in order from front to back, with practical exercises in each chapter encouraging you to look at your own business.

You may prefer to read it straight through and then go back and complete the exercises, or to do the exercises as you go along.

As you read, you'll be guided through different topics, with case studies and examples. Practical action points are included to help you tackle an issue in your own business, which you can easily refer back to if it arises again.

The book is intended as a practical tool to help you self-diagnose issues in your business. After reading it, if you can identify with certainty your main areas of improvement relating to profitability, then I'll have achieved my goal for writing this book.

How to avoid overwhelm

If you are very new to running a business, find numbers challenging or just know enough about yourself to understand that you are going to find it difficult to get through all the exercises, then I encourage you to look at Appendix 1, which is what I call "if you do nothing else".

This covers the bare minimum that you need to look at. The rewards of working all the way through the book are huge and will help you gain a deeper understanding of your business. But if you find yourself getting overwhelmed, it's better to do the "if you do nothing else" exercises than nothing at all.

Our case studies

To give more context to the concepts discussed in this book, I use three fictionalized characters to help illustrate the points.

Each character is entirely made up (and any resemblance to any real-life people or businesses is entirely coincidental), but they are an amalgamation of hundreds of conversations I've had over the years with product businesses of all sizes.

The case studies are three small snapshots into different types of product businesses – an independent bricks and mortar store, a small e-commerce store and a larger business selling via the web and wholesale.

They bring to life some of the common issues and challenges outlined in the book. Even if you are not sure what your underlying challenges are in your business, pay attention to the case studies.

If you feel like you recognize what they are talking about in terms of their challenges, then you should look in more detail at that particular chapter to see whether or not your tiger has some of the same characteristics as theirs. Let's meet them now.

Salma the shop owner

Salma has always dreamed of having her own shop. After taking voluntary redundancy, she opened her dream boutique in her home town in 2019. She lives in a pretty seaside town, which in a typical year gets many visitors during the summer months.

She loves being part of the local community, as well as everything to do with the creative side of running the shop. Salma has a great sense of style that helps her pick out just what her customers have come to know and love her for – stylish, affordable pieces to gift to yourself or others. She mostly works with local artists and small businesses, plus a few other suppliers that she has found at trade shows.

What Salma is not so fond of is balancing her numbers every month. With members of staff to pay, and rent, rates and increasingly expensive utilities to cover each month, she has a lot to manage.

Emmanuel the e-commerce seller

Emmanuel has a degree in product design, but after university took a job working in the civil service. His passion for design never left him though, and he started a blog about creating a design-led home as a hobby.

Over the years, he started to add some links to the blog to allow readers to purchase certain products from different websites. One day he realized that he could sell them himself. He switched the blog to a shoppable platform and started with a small range of highly curated products, eventually having a small range of products manufactured for him as well.

Emmanuel now has about 100 products on his site, including the items that he manufactures, as well as pieces from other businesses. He has recently moved to a fulfilment centre, finally getting his living room back!

Irene the illustrator

Irene spent 17 years in marketing, before a health scare made her re-evaluate her stressful job. With two small children and a wife who worked full time, they made the decision that Irene would leave her job and stay at home to help create more of a balance for the whole family.

Once her youngest child was at nursery, she started to think about ways that she could contribute to the family finances doing something she loved.

She began painting beautiful artwork for her friend's nurseries. They were so popular that she decided to open up an Etsy shop with prints of her artwork and cards, as well as taking a stall on her local craft market.

After a couple of years where sales rose steadily, Irene decided to wholesale her prints and cards and now has around 40 stockists. She still sells via Etsy but mostly drives traffic to her Shopify website.

Who am I and how can I help you?

I'd like to take a moment to introduce myself properly and explain exactly what my background is and why I'm writing this book.

I have worked in the retail industry since 2000, when my search for a graduate job led me to a description of merchandising.

It explained how merchandisers were highly numerate, looking at the figures behind a retail business – sales, stock and profitability. However, they also got to work alongside the buyers and designers, so took a more strategic look at products.

As soon as I read that description I knew that this was what I wanted to do, and for the next 17 years, I had a challenging but rewarding career. I worked across several retailers in the US and UK in multiple product areas, from womenswear to kidswear, fashion accessories and jewellery, skincare and baby products to stationery and art supplies.

The one thing the different retailers I worked for had in common was a total focus on creating or curating the best products.

True to the description that I read all those years ago, merchandising focuses on how creative ideas make money. I spent 17 years planning and strategizing sales, carefully monitoring profitability and keeping the stock moving.

When it became time for me to leave the corporate world and pursue my own business, I was curious to find out whether or not these skills that I had spent nearly two decades honing would work for the small businesses that I was drawn to work with.

Most people I spoke with had started their product business as a way of connecting with their creativity. Many of them had taken the time to educate themselves about running a small business, but what they had learnt was often generic advice rather than information aimed specifically at product businesses. As a result, as they grew, they were not prepared for the complexities of maintaining profit in a product business.

My experience with growing sales and profits for some of the biggest names on the high street was a perfect fit for what these business owners were lacking in their understanding. Over the last few years, I have worked as a consultant and mentor, created courses, given talks and workshops, spoken on podcasts and written thousands of words on how to plan and grow sales and profits for independent retailers and brands.

How big businesses think about profits

Although small businesses operate very differently to big retail chains, it's useful to know how the bigger retailers focus on profits. It's fair to say that there is a much stronger emphasis on sales, stock and profits in bigger companies. They are reviewing these numbers on a weekly, if not daily, basis.

Each month, I'd have to update the finance team with an estimate on the "in-margin", or the percentage profit that we were expecting our stock to hit that month. We'd also have to declare how much stock we were expecting into the business, as well as our future purchasing plans.

Other key metrics that were closely monitored were the amount of money we spent on promotions and marking down stock, and what percentage of sales came from our full-price sales as opposed to sales made with a discount. Stock was equally monitored obsessively.

The slightest shift or variation from the original plan could have major implications for the bottom line of the company. I remember watching as the Chief Financial Officer in one company I worked for illustrated how a small fluctuation in our exchange rate, which made purchasing products from overseas a few percentage points more expensive, had just wiped millions of pounds of profit off the forecast bottom line for the business that year.

This is the world that I was immersed in for nearly two decades. A world that is highly governed by the numbers, with profitability kept in sharp focus.

While I vastly prefer working with small and medium-sized businesses, and find the passion, energy and innovation of this sector of the retail industry highly motivating, there are some aspects of the way that bigger businesses are run that small businesses could benefit from.

That's what I aim to do with this book. I want to take some of those big business learnings and help you apply them to your small business. The combination of small business passion and big business discipline is a powerful recipe for success.

Key points

- Because of the unique challenges of running a product business, in particular the challenges of managing stock, it is easy to find yourself with a product business that you don't feel comfortable with.
- After working through the exercises in this book, you'll feel more in control of your numbers, clear about what you want to be measuring and more confident about managing your tiger.
- We'll be using a series of fictionalized case studies to examine the issues more closely.
- Everything in this book is drawing on my experience of more than two decades in the retail industry.
- Details of bonus materials can be found in the 'Additional resources' section at the end of the book.

CHAPTER 2

THE ANATOMY OF A TIGER

From working with business owners over the last few years, I've found that while people may not often be able to self-diagnose where the problem lies in their business, they are able to describe how their business is making them feel.

In this chapter, we're going to look in more detail at how tiger businesses make people feel, why they are so common and what makes up their anatomy.

Our case studies

Salma the shop owner

Running my own shop has been such a big learning curve. Stock is something that I struggle with and cash flow is a constant battle.

We have a lot of local artists who stock with us on a "sale or return" basis, where I display their stock and take a 20% commission off any sales that I make. In theory, this is ideal because it means we don't pay to have the stock in the store; we only pay when it sells.

In reality, at the end of each month, I always have to pay an amount of money out of my sales to the sale or return artists, which never seems to leave enough for me. I also spend hours on paperwork, which is frustrating.

I feel like I'm on a treadmill. As soon as money comes in, it just goes straight out again.

Emmanuel the e-commerce seller

I have to place large orders at a time for each of my products, which means that I have to tie up a lot of cash at the same time. That used to be OK, but now that I'm VAT registered and I have the fulfilment centre, it feels like I'm making less and less on each item. As a result, I have to be incredibly careful with my cash flow.

It feels unpredictable. Sometimes I feel like I'm having a good month and then end up having some real problems with my cash flow. Other times it feels a bit quieter but I am covering my costs. I feel like I'm winging it most of the time.

Irene the illustrator

For a long time, I wasn't too worried about much in the business. I was always in profit and as long as my sales were going up, I didn't think too much about my bottom line.

Recently, with more and more expenses in my business, from the studio to the team members and the costs associated with those, I have found myself increasingly worried about the profit.

If I have even one quiet day, I immediately start asking myself whether I'm going to have enough money to cover all of my expenses. I can't quite seem to get a handle on what my sales need to be for the new costs that I have.

I thought it would get easier the more that I grow, but I feel way more stressed than I was at the beginning when it was just me and my paintbrush.

Although each of these business owners has a different model and way of selling their products, they all share some of the same characteristics of a tiger business – nervousness, uncertainty about what to do for the best and lack of visibility around how to make the next best move.

Why do product businesses become tigers?

One thing makes product businesses so uniquely challenging and so prone to becoming unnerving tigers, and that's stock.

When starting your own business, a product business is one of the most scalable options. Once you've figured out what you want to sell, who you want to sell it to and, most importantly, what those people want to buy, you can keep growing by selling more. And not just grow a little bit; you can keep adding stores, or channels or routes to market until you end up with annual sales of over $500 billion like Walmart, one of the biggest retailers in the world.

In other words, there is no limit to how big your business can grow, if that's what you want. But you have to learn to overcome a series of challenges along the way. It's those challenges that turn many product businesses into cash-hungry tigers that leave their owners feeling off-balance and uncertain.

How do you deal with tigers?

In this book, I outline three places in your business that you can look at to help you tame the tiger it has become. We look in depth at these different parts of the tiger-business anatomy – the teeth, tail and stomach.

The teeth

This is the first place to look if you think you have a tiger not a tabby cat. How big of a bite is taken out of your revenue with each sale?

If you sell an item for £12, and after tax and expenses are left with £7.50 for yourself, your business is going to feel different to one where there is only £2.50 left after all tax and expenses.

Understanding what that looks like for your business and how to manage and measure it will go a long way towards making sure that the teeth and the bite are under control.

A bite involves two things – the top teeth and the bottom teeth. We're going to look at your "in-margin" (the top teeth) in Chapter 3, or the amount of money that gets taken out by product costs, and the "out-margin" (the bottom teeth) in Chapter 4, the actual margin that you are achieving on your sales once any discounts, selling fees and postage costs are accounted for.

The tail

How big of a tail does your business have? If you're wondering what on earth I'm talking about, the tail is the name given in retail to the unproductive stock in your business.

You may well have heard of the 80/20 rule or the Pareto principle. In a product business, it refers to the common phenomenon that 80% of your sales will be coming from just 20% of your products. On the other hand, it also means that 20% of your sales will be coming from the remaining 80% of your products.

That 80% is known as the tail. And having too much stock of those unproductive products is one of the quickest ways to lock up too much cash in your business and create an unwieldy tiger. The bigger the tail, the bigger the tiger. In Chapter 5, we'll look in more detail at how you can analyse this tail.

We're also going to examine in Chapter 6 how you answer that difficult question "how much stock should I have?", so that you can set your stock levels accordingly.

The stomach

The third place to look at to understand more about your tiger is how much you are feeding it.

Tiger businesses are hungry beasts: you may find that as soon as money comes in through sales, it goes straight out again on stock and other expenses. Looking at the tail and reducing its size will help with this issue, but the other area you need to understand is how much you are feeding the tiger in terms of fixed costs.

Most of the time when I work with product businesses, the issue usually comes from the teeth or the tail. Sometimes though, especially as a business grows, there's a problem with the amount of other expenses.

If your business has too many fixed expenses, for example staffing, agency fees or premises, it is very difficult to grow profitably. In Chapter 7 we will create a framework to help you live within your means as a business owner.

Isn't the answer just to sell more?

You may be reading this and thinking to yourself, surely she's missing the point? Surely if your product business isn't producing enough cash, the answer is to sell more?

Well, yes and no.

More sales help you specifically if your fixed costs are too high for your overall sales. Let's say you have a studio and it costs you £1,000 a month. Your sales are around £1,500 a month, but after you take out taxes and product costs, you're only generating £650 of profit; each month you will be making a loss.

If you can double your sales and stay at the same sales-to-profit ratio, then you will go from being unprofitable to profitable.

However, if your main issue is the teeth, the more you sell, the more you'll be spinning your wheels. Growing sales means more people to employ, more storage space or bigger facilities, more packaging, often more stock. If you are under-profitable with small sales, as you grow, that won't change. Without visibility of key numbers, sleepwalking into lower profits is a real possibility for product businesses.

Similarly with the stock issue, unless you keep an eye on that tail as you grow, it will also grow along with you. And remember, the bigger the tail, the bigger the tiger. I've worked with several fast-growth businesses who haven't paid close enough attention to their amount of stock, causing a major problem as sales increased.

Yes, more sales is a very important part of growing and developing your business. However, as we'll examine later in the book in Chapter 8, it's only part of the story.

It's entirely possible to have a six-figure, or even a seven-, eight-, nine- or ten-figure product business that makes NO money. Believe me, I've worked with, or for, several. But here's the good news – the more you learn and practise these principles, the more well equipped you'll be as your business grows to understand the pressures, the pain points and, ultimately, how to keep that tiger under control.

How is this book going to help you tame your tiger?

The exercises in this book will help you examine these three elements – the teeth, tail and stomach – in your business, and identify where any problems might lie. That is the first step, and arguably the most important one in this whole process – helping you self-diagnose what's going on in your business.

This book will also help you to start to measure and understand more about these different elements. You'll be able to go from having a bad feeling about how much money you are making to being able to clearly identify what the issue is and where it's coming from.

Partly this is knowing what numbers you should be tracking on a monthly basis. Chapter 9 helps you create a plan to keep on top of your key numbers.

Finally, once you have identified the problem and measured it, you can then put together a plan to make improvements. Once you have that plan in place, and an understanding of how to work with it on an ongoing basis, then you'll have truly tamed your tiger.

With that in mind, the best option for you to get to grips with your tiger is to start by examining each of the elements in turn. And that means starting with the teeth.

Key points

- Tigers feel scary as we aren't trained to recognize or manage them.
- The three areas that we need to look at and measure are:
    - the teeth – how big of a bite is being taken out of our sales;
    - the tail – how much unproductive stock is trapped in our business;
    - the stomach – how much we are feeding the beast.
- Growing sales alone without understanding and managing these other elements is not sufficient to alleviate financial stress in your business.

Over to you

Spend a few moments thinking about the following questions in relation to your own business.

1. How are you feeling right now? Do you recognize any of the descriptions of how tiger businesses make you feel?

2. Do any of the stories from Salma, Emmanuel and Irene sound familiar to you? What parts do you relate to?

3. What makes you feel nervous? Can you put your finger on what is making you feel uncomfortable?

4. Do you have any thoughts about where your problem might be? When you read the descriptions of teeth, tail and stomach, did any of them feel like they might be an issue?

CHAPTER 3

THE BITE – THE TOP TEETH

We've identified what makes a tiger business, how it feels and the key numbers that you need to understand and tame your tiger.

In this chapter and Chapter 4, we're going to examine in more detail the first element of the tiger – its teeth.

The teeth matter because they affect the "bite". This refers to the size of the bite that your costs are taking out of your prices, also known as your profit margin. In this chapter, we'll examine what the bite is, why it's so important and look in detail at how you calculate it, focusing particularly on the in-margin or "top teeth".

Before you start this chapter, go to www.resilientretailclub. com/tigertookit to get your free margin calculator, which will help as you work through the examples and your own margins.

Our case studies

Salma the shop owner

One of the biggest challenges that I have as a shop is that I don't make or manufacture my own products, so everything that I sell comes from someone else. Because of this, I am only ever going to be able to make a 50% margin maximum.

In the shop itself, what is tough is all the sale or return items that I have. I get just 20% of the sale price for each one of these items and that's depressing. If I sell a £20 item, I'm getting just £4 at the end of the day, which barely covers the time it takes to put together all of the paperwork to reimburse the artist at the end of the month, plus I have to pay VAT on that £4. Not to mention the work of selling the item, storing it and displaying it as well.

Sometimes I feel like we have a decent turnover, but when I look at what is left at the end of the month, it doesn't seem anything like enough compared to what I think it should be. We have good footfall, the local community gets behind what we are offering, but I often end up feeling resentful when I look at how much we're keeping from our sales.

Emmanuel the e-commerce seller

I buy the majority of my products from other businesses, so I have a maximum of 50% margin on most things. At least, I think I do! I'm not that disciplined when it comes to checking my margins; I just see what I like and buy it. The only exception is on my own manufactured products – I can comfortably make about 70% margin on those items.

It did make me feel very nervous when I registered for VAT, and I've sort of stuck my head in the sand. I know that my margins have dropped, but not by how much.

Irene the illustrator

This is the one area I feel confident about! My margins are mostly fantastic on my paper goods. I can easily hit 75–80% on some of my prints, especially if it's a popular one that I order in volume.

I'm not sure how it will affect me in the future though, especially since I want to branch out into more products including ceramics and enamelware, and I know they will have lower margins.

What is the bite?

Let's delve into a little more detail about the bite, and start off with considering this fact about your business.

> *There is only one place in your business that you generate money – the difference between what you pay for your stock and what you sell it for.*

Think for a moment about a big retailer like Marks & Spencer. Their business costs are enormous – a recent annual report showed costs of over £236 million. These costs cover everything they need to operate, from thousands of staff to hundreds of stores with associated rent, fleets of lorries, giant warehouses and millions of pounds worth of stock.

All of those costs have to be covered from one place – the difference between what they pay for their stock and what they sell it for. Yes, they may have small amounts of additional income from some services and other such activities, but the vast majority of their money has to come from that difference. In retail terms, this is known as the profit margin, or sometimes as RGP (retail gross product).

If that difference shrinks because the prices that they are paying go up, or because the amount they are selling for on average goes down (for example, if they sell less at full price and more at clearance), then there is less money flowing through the business to cover those costs.

The retail industry in general operates on wafer-thin profits as a percentage of sales, despite starting with what seem like very high profit margins. For example, it would not be unusual for a big retailer to have a target intake margin of 75% plus, so an item that was sold for £12 would have been bought for £2.50 or less.

People are often shocked to hear those numbers, and may even consider these prices to be exploitative. However, bear in mind all of the costs that have to be covered. Despite this high starting point, the average high street retailer makes on average 1–2% profit as a percentage of net sales (after VAT is removed). That would mean that a business turning over £120 million would make a profit of £1–2 million once VAT is removed and all of the other costs are taken into account.

This is also what was behind the collapse of many of the big high street retailers that we have seen disappear over the last few years. As the Centre for Retail Research note, 180 large retailers have gone out of business in the last five years with a loss of nearly a quarter of a million jobs.[1]

Although many blame the rise of online shopping, I believe that many of the businesses were the victims of rising costs. Their whole business model was based on purchasing from the Far East in large volumes at low costs, and shipping across the world to sell in stores. With costs going up in China and other countries, as well as increases in the costs of raw materials, transportation and fluctuations in exchange

---

[1] Centre for Retail Research (2022). 'Who's gone bust in UK retailing in 2019–2022?' Available from www.retailresearch.org/whos-gone-bust-retail.html [accessed 13 August 2022].

rates, UK retailers were hit with many cost increases simultaneously.

Factor in the (very necessary) increases in living wages, business rates and costs associated with running shops in the UK, it's not surprising that anyone who was teetering at around 1–3% profit as a percentage of sales would quickly tip into the red.

Why am I telling you this? As proof of the importance of profit in retail businesses and how it can literally make or break your business.

The same concept applies to your small business. Every cost that you have in your business, including your rent, advertising, staff costs, the salary you want to pay yourself or anything else that you can think of, has to be covered by the difference between what you pay to buy or make your products and what you sell them for.

Luckily for you, the costs associated with running a small business are typically lower than the huge costs that big retailers have to cover, but the problem is that your profit margins are typically much lower too, since you don't have the power to buy in bulk like a big retailer.

That is why it is so important to understand what your profit margins are, and to be able to understand what they need to be for your business to succeed. It is the foundation of your business. If your topline grows without enough attention to what is happening with your profits, it's entirely possible to have a business with a large and growing turnover that isn't making any money.

In this chapter, we're going to break down how to calculate your profit margin and what to do when the numbers don't add up.

Calculating your profit margin – the two elements

There are two different elements to your profit margin – in-margin and out-margin – and both are worth monitoring within your business. The in-margin relates to the relationship between your cost price and planned selling price, while the out-margin looks at your cost price and what you **actually** sold something for, taking into account any discounts. If you think about your tiger, they are like the top teeth and the bottom teeth that make up the bite.

It's easy to remember which is which, as it relates to the process of sourcing and selling goods.

The product is purchased by you, coming **in** to your business. The price that you pay for this item compared to what you are **planning** on selling it for is your **in-margin**.

It is then sold by you to a customer, so it's going **out** of the business. The difference between what you paid for this product and what you **actually** sold it for, including any discounts, is your **out-margin**.

We will discuss the out-margin in Chapter 4, but in this chapter let's focus on the in-margin.

Your in-margin

In big retailers, there are whole teams of people who obsess over the in-margin. It was one of the numbers I had to report to the finance team when I worked for big retailers.

You have to be obsessed too and it starts with the following process. For every single product that you sell, work out how much money you have made after all of the costs.

If you have a large collection of products, or if you just know that you will never make the time to sit down and go through all of your products, make sure at the bare minimum you look at the profit margin on your best-selling items, as this will make the biggest difference to your bottom line.

The profit margin is the percentage of the selling price that is profit. So, if you sell a £10 product and make £7 profit, your profit margin is 70% (assuming that you are not VAT registered).

Once you have taken any applicable taxes and costs away from your selling price, you can then work out what percentage your remaining profit is compared to the original selling price.

The calculation in full looks like this:

In-margin (non-VAT-registered businesses) =
(selling price – total product costs)/selling price × 100

In-margin (20% VAT-registered businesses) =
((selling price/1.2) – total product costs)/
(selling price/1.2) × 100

Not sure if you should be looking at the VAT or non-VAT calculation? This is discussed in more detail later in the chapter.

As a rule of thumb, your in-margin should be at least 50% if you are selling directly to your customers and closer to 70% or higher if you want to sell wholesale to other retailers. Just to clarify, when you are selling at wholesale, your margin won't be anywhere close to 70%, but if the margin you achieve at your retail price is 70% or higher, then you can be confident that your wholesale activities will make you money.

Ultimately though, you need to track your profit margin on an ongoing basis, and look at how you can increase it over time. The higher that number is, the easier your cash flow will be.

If you are selling other people's products, in other words buying from another business, you are unlikely to make more than 50% in-margin as most wholesale pricing is set up to give the retailer a 50% margin when they sell to the final customer.

Factor in every cost

Factor in every cost to accurately calculate the profit margin. One of the most common mistakes I see product businesses make is that they factor in the cost of the materials, but forget that they cover the postage. They forget to factor in the cost of their own time that they took to make the item. They forget that they send each order wrapped in a beautiful glossy box with a gorgeous ribbon on, which can end up costing as much as the item in the box.

I have even seen a major high street retailer who didn't look at how much it cost to ship their beautiful cushions in from the Far East. When they ran the numbers, it turned out that they didn't make *any* money on those items!

Someone spent hours designing them; people worked with the supplier to have them manufactured; they were packed up, shipped over, sent out to stores; the sales people spent time explaining how great they were; and when the customer took it home, the retailer made *no* money! In fact, they would have made *more* money if they didn't even sell the cushions!

Now, they had other products making them money, so this mistake didn't kill them. How long could you survive if it turned out that you weren't making any money on what you were selling?

Here are some of the costs that should be included in your margin calculation.

For manufactured goods:

- What it costs to buy the product.
- Any costs to get the product to you – for example, shipping and import duties.
- The cost of any packaging, including tissue paper, stickers, boxes and so on.
- The cost of postage to get the product to the customer – unless they are paying this.
- Fulfilment costs – how much is it costing you to have it packed up and dispatched? If you are the person doing this job, what is your time worth?

For handmade goods:

- What it costs to buy the materials to make the product.
- Any costs to get the materials to you – for example, shipping and import duties.
- The cost of any packaging, including tissue paper, stickers, boxes and so on.
- The cost of postage to get the product to the customer – unless they are paying this.
- Fulfilment costs – how much is it costing you to have it packed up and dispatched? If you are the person doing this job, what is your time worth?
- Your time to make the product.

Factoring in the cost of the time taken to make and/or pack the product is important, and a lot of small businesses struggle with this to start off. It's important to factor in these costs, otherwise, as you grow, you will never have enough profit in each item to outsource packing or making.

Depending on your business model, you may also want to include your selling fees (for example, PayPal commission) in your in-margin calculation – they impact every transaction so it's useful to see how they affect your margin. However, if you sell across lots of different platforms and so have lots of different levels of fees, I suggest looking at your selling fees when you come to examine your out-margin in Chapter 4.

Running your profit margin calculation for every item is an important task in your business. Ideally, you should analyse your profit margin on every item before you agree to purchase or decide to make it. Here are a couple more examples to illustrate the point.

Irene's blanket

When Irene was first starting out, one of her products was a wool blanket for a baby; this item complemented her nursery print designs and retailed at £180 each. She was not VAT registered when she made them. She bought the wool at a price of £30 for enough to make three blankets, including shipping and taxes. Labels were £10 for 100. Each blanket took four hours to make, and she decided to factor in £12.50 an hour for making.

The blankets were wrapped in five sheets of tissue paper, which cost £5 for 100 sheets, and each one was shipped to the customers in a glossy branded box, which cost £150 for 10. Shipping to the customer was £15 for registered delivery, but customers paid that cost. How do you calculate how much profit she was making on each item?

One of the issues that many businesses face is that they don't often see a single-unit price for their products. Prices come in across multiple invoices, and so unless you stop and work out each unit price individually, it can be hard to unpick how much you are making on a sale.

In the example above, the wool and shipping costs were £30, so if that's enough for three blankets, the cost per blanket was £30 divided by 3, or £10.

Labels were 10p each (£10 divided by 100). Labour costs were £50. Tissue was 25p (£5 divided by 100 is 5p, and she used five sheets), the box was £15.

Total costs were £10 + £0.10 + £50 + £0.25 + £15 = £75.35

If she sold it for £180, then her profit was £180 minus £75.35, which is £104.65, or 58%.

Here it is in table form:

Wool	£10.00
Labels	£0.10
Labour	£50.00
Box	£15.00
Tissue	£0.25
Total costs	£75.35
Selling price	£180.00
Net sales – after VAT is removed (this is the same as the selling price as she paid no VAT at this point)	£180.00
Profit	£104.65
% of what she keeps	58.14%

Emmanuel's containers

Let's look at another example using a manufactured product. Emmanuel is VAT registered and imports stainless-steel food containers manufactured by a small factory. A small container sells for £15. He pays £1.00 per container to the manufacturer.

Shipping and duty is £150 for a shipment that contains 300 containers. He sends the containers out to customers in a plain cardboard box, which he buys in batches of 100 for £30.

The fulfilment centre he works with charges him £1 to pick each item. He does not charge the customer shipping, but it costs him £2.20. How much profit is he making on each item? Broken down to one item, the numbers look like this:

Container	£1.00
Shipping and duty	£0.50
Box	£0.30
Postage to customer	£2.20
Picking fee	£1.00
Total costs	£5.00
Selling price	£15.00
He keeps (after VAT)	£12.50
Profit	£7.50
% of what he keeps	60.00%

The key element in both calculations is that the business owners have looked at all of the costs associated with making a product and broken them down to the level of one item. They can now see exactly what their in-margin is for each product.

Dealing with fluctuations

As freight costs soar and exchange rates are volatile, you may be wondering how to deal with fluctuations in costs such as shipping, duty or the cost of the item if the exchange rate varies.

Big retailers have to work with this on a daily basis, and there are a few ways of dealing with it. My preferred method is to use a worst-case scenario number for your calculations, so that it's possible that the reality will be better. For example, you have noticed that freight prices have increased by 20%, and when you forecast forward then you increase them by another 20% to see what that looks like.

The same goes for exchange rates. Pick one that is perhaps slightly worse than what you typically pay, or maybe the worst from the last 12 months. This will again help you calculate a worst-case scenario.

When prices are moving quickly, you'll need to keep checking your figures to make sure that things haven't got even worse than your worst projection. In general, if you go with what you think is a realistic, or even a pessimistic, view of your costs, then that should help keep you out of trouble.

What not to include in the margin calculation

Some schools of thought suggest breaking down your overheads such as your rent or utilities into a cost per unit to include in your profit margins; however, I find this counterintuitive.

On this basis, the more you sell, the smaller that cost per unit would be, so you'd need to constantly be re-evaluating this number as your sales changed.

We will be dealing with fixed costs in much more detail in Chapter 7, but for now, just know that I suggest keeping all non-product costs separate from your profit margin calculation.

Not sure if it's a product cost or not? Ask yourself, if I sold twice as many, would this cost increase? If they would, it's probably a product cost. If not, assume it is a fixed cost to be examined later on.

Looking at "one-off" costs

What is trickier to consider are the "one-off" costs associated with each product. For example, let's say that you pay a designer £100 to create an art print for you. In a sense, that is a product cost rather than a business overhead, so do you add that to the unit cost?

There are a couple of options here and which one you choose depends on how you find it most straightforward to think about your business.

Option 1 – Look at these costs, which could include product photography, set-up costs or design fees, as an ongoing overhead that is part of the cost of doing business. They will then factor into any break-even calculations that you do.

Option 2 – For the first order that you place for an item, break down the cost. So, if you paid £100 for the design of a print, and then printed 100 of them, you would add £1 to each print to cover that fee.

For future orders, you can calculate the margin without these one-off costs. Reorders in general are more profitable than the first order that you have, and it's worth being able to see that easily. Even if you don't pay design fees for an item, there is generally less work and less photography costs involved in bringing back an item you have previously sold.

The benefit to this approach is that it allows you to correctly assess which is the right choice between creating new products and reordering existing ones.

It can also highlight issues in the business. For example, if you have to spend £50 on photography for an item, and you are only ever going to sell three of them, clearly you will not be very profitable. In that way, breaking down your one-off costs gives you a much more accurate representation of what's going on in the business.

Value Added Tax

Before I say any more about Value Added Tax (VAT), it is important that I remind you to speak with your accountant about anything tax related, so that you can be sure to get tailored advice specific to your unique situation. I'm going to share with you some general information about the way VAT impacts product businesses as they grow. It is not a substitute for professional advice.

VAT or Value Added Tax registration is an important milestone in any business journey. It comes when the business hits £85,000 turnover in a rolling 12-month period. Because of this, it's important to not only look at how many sales you make each month, but at what the rolling 12-month sales are, to understand how close you are getting to the VAT limit.

Not all businesses are impacted by VAT. There are lots of different rules about what is and isn't included. For example, baby and children's clothes, some food and printed materials aren't included, and there are other exceptions too.

I am not going to attempt to go into great detail about VAT in this section. All I want to do is show you how your profit calculation changes as you become VAT registered.

Let's revisit the first example:

Before she was VAT registered, Irene made blankets that she retailed for £180 each. She bought the wool at a price of £30 for enough to make three blankets, including shipping and taxes. Labels were £10 for 100. Each blanket took four hours to make, and she decided to pay herself £12.50 an hour. The blankets were wrapped in five sheets of tissue paper, which cost £5 for 100 sheets, and each one was shipped to the customers in a glossy branded box, which cost £150 for 10. Shipping to the customer was £15 for registered delivery, but customers paid that cost.

Let's take a look at how that changes before and after VAT:

	Before and after VAT	
	Before	After
Wool	£10.00	£8.33
Labels	£0.10	£0.08
Labour	£50.00	£50.00
Box	£15.00	£12.50
Tissue	£0.25	£0.21
Total costs	£75.35	£71.13

Selling price	£180.00	£180.00
She keeps	£180.00	£150.00
Profit	£104.65	£78.88
% of what she keeps	58.14%	52.58%

The impact of hitting the VAT limit is significant, and it's often a real nail-biting moment for small businesses.

You will notice, however, that some of this shift is offset by reduced costs. VAT is a balancing tax; in other words, any VAT that you pay on supplies is balanced against the VAT that you owe the government based on your sales. You can disregard any VAT that you are paying on your supplies as it will net off against the VAT from sales.

In the example above, Irene was paying VAT on her wool, labels, boxes and tissue paper so she was able to remove those from her profit-margin calculation as she became VAT registered.

The points to remember are:

1. The best way to go through the VAT limit is clearly, and with forward planning.

2. You will receive some reduction in your costs if you pay for any items that have VAT on them.

3. As with anything related to tax, it's important to have a discussion with your accountant to make sure that you have the most accurate information that relates to your business.

4. Many business owners find that approaching the VAT limit is a good point at which to reassess their pricing

and make sure that it is still profitable enough after they have to apply VAT.

5. Alternatively, some people prefer to set up their prices to accommodate VAT right from the very beginning of their business, so that they enjoy higher profits while they are building towards the VAT limit, but can absorb the VAT at a later stage.

Staying up to date

Unfortunately, as nice as it would be to only have to calculate your margins once, in an era of rising costs, you need to be aware of the most current prices for your products or materials.

Because we often receive invoices for various elements of our products separately, for example receiving a packaging invoice separately from invoices for other items that make up a product, it's easy to miss where costs are creeping up.

If you have your margins set up on a margin calculator such as the one that you can download as part of your Tiger Tamer's Toolkit at www.resilientretailclub.com/tigertoolkit, then a good habit to get into is to double check each invoice that you receive and how that affects your margin.

If you used to pay £4 for the fabric you need to make a pair of children's leggings, but then when you receive the invoice it's now £5, that is important information to keep a note of. A margin calculator will allow you to update your margins with the latest figures so that you are fully aware of your latest position.

What to do if the numbers aren't good?

What happens if you run your numbers only to discover that your margins are not that great? This is a common situation that many small business owners find themselves in. There are a few different options for how to move forward.

Negotiate with suppliers

If you work with a particular supplier, especially if you have done so for a few months or longer, it may well be worth speaking to them about your pricing. One of the most effective ways of doing this is framing your question in the following way.

"I have been reviewing my margins, and in an ideal world I'd be paying X for this item. What would it take for me to get that price?"

Sometimes the answer will be that they can't ever accommodate that price. Sometimes they'll give you options.

- Do you have to commit to more upfront? It's sometimes possible to negotiate a better deal if you commit to a certain amount. You don't always have to take all of that stock at the same time; it could be a firm commitment to take that amount across the whole year is enough for them to agree to give you a better price.
- Maybe they'll give you a better price if you pay upfront (if you're not paying upfront already).
- Sometimes they might make suggestions on how you can tweak the product in order to bring it in at the price you want it to be.

All of these are real possibilities, so it's worth asking that question. However, use your judgement carefully. If they are offering a better price per unit for larger quantities, it may not be the right decision for you to take it. You should always balance lower costs per unit against the impact that this will have on your cash flow, not to mention the difficulties that might arise in storing extra products!

Another factor to consider is how long it takes to sell that amount of stock. If you think that you could clear that amount in a few months, that's one thing. But buying years' worth of stock just to get a better unit price is not ideal.

These questions are still relevant if you are buying from other businesses on a wholesale basis. And they are also relevant if you are buying from another business on a different pricing structure such as sale or return. If you want to improve your margins on those types of products, then you can ask the same question: "What would it take to achieve this price?"

For some businesses that you are buying from on sale or return, you may be able to renegotiate the terms of the sale, in other words, get the items at wholesale prices if you commit and pay upfront. It may save both you and them time and hassle in paperwork and back and forth over sales.

Cross-costing

Cross-costing is the retail term for price checking against different suppliers. It's a worthwhile exercise, even if you are happy with your current supplier. It also helps avoid having all your eggs in one supplier basket.

If you have low margins because the product, or one of the elements of your product, is too expensive, it's definitely worth taking the time to get quotes from other suppliers. Even if you remain with your existing supplier, the best time to find an alternative supplier is when you are not in urgent need.

Finding someone you trust, working through the sampling process and building up enough of a relationship to order from them can take a long time, so it's better to have done some of the research and thought process beforehand.

Blended margins

If you have certain products that are strong sellers but have poor margins, is it possible to combine them together with other items to give you a better overall margin? This is known as a blended margin, and it can be a useful way to push up the profitability in your business.

Let's say Emmanuel has a beautiful tea towel that he sells in his shop. It is very popular but because of the way it is made (hand-dyed in India and then embroidered), it is expensive for him to buy in. Emmanuel decides to combine this tea towel with a set of his stainless-steel food containers (high margin) to create a gift set that is on average in his target margin range.

Reverse engineering

If you are happy with your prices, but the profits aren't high enough, ask yourself if there is anything you can do to reverse engineer items into a better profit margin.

Let's say that Emmanuel has a "new home" gift bundle on his website. It sells for £60. He wants to make a 60% margin on this item.

The formula for a target cost price is as follows:

> Target cost price (non-VAT-registered businesses) = retail price × (1 – ideal margin)
>
> Target cost price (20% VAT-registered businesses) = (retail price/1.2) × (1 – ideal margin)

In the example above, the calculation would look like this:

Target cost price (20% VAT-registered businesses)
= (retail price/1.2) × (1 – ideal margin)

$= (\text{£}60/1.2) \times (1 - 60\%)$
$= \text{£}50 \times 40\%$
$= \text{£}20$ target cost price.

With this in mind, he can then look at the items that make up the box, and make sure the cost price for that bundle comes in at no more than £20.

Similarly, if Irene is creating a cushion from her artwork, she can set a target cost price based on her selling price and the amount of money that she needs to be paying. This can help with negotiation.

Let's say she is going to sell a cushion for £75, she is VAT registered and wants to achieve a 65% margin.

Using the formula above, she calculates that her target cost price is:

Target cost price (20% VAT-registered businesses)
$= (\text{retail price}/1.2) \times (1 - \text{ideal margin})$ $(\text{£}75/1.2) \times (1 - 65\%)$
$= \text{£}62.50 \times 35\% = \text{£}21.88$

Imagine she gets a quote from a supplier for a cushion with tassels and piping, silk backing and hand embroidery picking out elements of the design. The quote is for £29 per cushion.

With a target cost price in mind, she can work with the supplier to understand what could be removed from the product.

What's the price without the tassels? Is there a cheaper way to finish the edges that isn't piping? What if instead of silk she used cotton? How much would it cost to reduce or remove the embroidery?

The supplier will not, in general, be offended by these types of questions. These are the types of discussions that happen hundreds of times a day in big retailers.

For example, fashion retailers will play around with the amount and spacing of embroidery and other embellishments, the composition of the fabric used, the construction of the garment, the hem circumference and amount of fabric being used. All of these things will be picked apart to create a garment that fits into the margin requirements, not the other way around.

My biggest rule of thumb in these situations is making sure that you are not impacting the quality of the product, and you aren't removing something that makes you unique or is part of your business DNA.

For example, if your entire business is built on an ethos of minimizing your environmental impact and supporting organic cotton, clearly switching your organic cotton for standard cotton will not work. You will have to look at other elements instead.

Focusing on your pricing and then working into the cost price will help you home in on where you can cut costs but still offer your customer something they want.

Please note, if you are manufacturing, it is NOT a good idea to share your target cost price directly with your supplier, especially at the beginning of your negotiation.

The first price you want to get from them should be based on **their** calculations, not what you give them as a target. That's because it's possible that their price would be lower than your target. If they already know your target, even if it will cost them less to make the product, there's a chance they'll just tell you that they can hit your target price. Keep it private, at least to start with.

First price, right price – how to evaluate your pricing

You'll notice that so far I haven't mentioned anything about raising prices if your margins aren't high enough. That's because it should be your last resort after looking at every other way to improve your in-margin.

Having said that, part of having an effective profitable business does rely on you being on top of your pricing. That means reviewing them regularly and looking at where you might be able to increase them, responding to product cost increases and monitoring what needs to be adjusted.

For some businesses, reviewing prices will be an easy exercise because you buy products from another business, in which case you will have a list of recommended retail prices, or RRPs.

For those that set their own prices, this part can be a minefield. It is often one of the hardest tasks for businesses who are first starting out, because pricing inadvertently reflects your beliefs about yourself and your business.

Subconsciously, pricing challenges your thoughts about money and what you think you can charge for different products. You've got to try and set a price that makes you feel comfortable. Working out the price is part art and part science but there are a few basic principles that are important to apply.

Your pricing is absolutely critical. Make sure you get it right. Don't assume that you'll only make a sale if you charge less for your products. If you underprice your products significantly, you can affect how your customers think about your products – especially in terms of quality as that leads to customers making assumptions. On top of that, it's very hard to have anything resembling a profitable business if you are chronically undercharging for your goods.

The best approach is to work through a logical process to ensure that your prices are correct for your customer and your competitive market. Once you have done these exercises, then you can check your profitability.

Many established business owners would also benefit from a regular pricing review, at the very least once a year. This allows them to re-examine their costs and look at where they have crept up over time, as well as check in with what their competitors are doing. Let's review a three-step process for setting prices below:

Learn from competitors

No business operates in isolation, so be aware of the market price for your products. The first step when it comes to setting your prices is to analyse what your competitors are doing. Look at their pricing to help you build a benchmark for your own product pricing.

Every large retailer will spend a number of days a year going out and looking at what their competitors are doing, as well as reviewing their websites. It's an important process in the industry and can be a very valuable way of understanding how you measure up.

The trap that many small businesses fall into here is that they compare themselves to the wrong kind of competitor. They look at a big supermarket and see that they sell a T-shirt for £5, and wonder how they can compete with that price.

The simple answer? They can't. But that's OK. People have many reasons for buying from supermarkets, just like they have different reasons for buying from small businesses. Setting your prices compared to competitors requires looking at people who share a similar business model to you.

Can you find three other businesses that sell similar products to you, produced in a similar way? If you hand-pour your soy wax candles, look for three other businesses that do the same. If your clothes are made from organic cotton in a small factory in Portugal, who else does that?

Don't worry about the aesthetics of the other products – it doesn't matter if they are all about bright prints and you're all about Scandi minimalism. Unless it's something that will impact the pricing, for example you are all about heavily embellished hand-embroidered fabrics and they use plain cotton (in which case I'd argue you need different competitors for your comparison), you can disregard differences in the look of the actual product itself.

Once you have found the correct competitors to give you a comparison, however, you don't have to match their prices exactly. You can have your own pricing and it can even be a point of differentiation between you and your competition.

If you haven't checked your competitors' pricing recently, it's worth another look. Many people I have spoken to found that they were making assumptions about what the market price is for the products that they sell without updating their information. When they actually checked, their competitors had increased their prices. When prices are rising, it's important to keep your competitor information updated.

Ask your customers

When was the last time that you sat down with your ideal customer to chat about their buying habits? The next step after reviewing your competitors' prices is to make sure that you are cross-referencing what your customers typically pay.

Ask people what they have bought in the past instead of asking them if they would pay a certain amount of money for an item, as people tend to be aspirational in their answers.

In other words, if you say, "Would you pay £125 for this T-shirt?" they are most likely to answer "Yes", but if you ask them "How much were the last three T-shirts you bought?" and they say £20–£25, then you have a better idea of the real prices they are prepared to pay.

Don't forget to ask them about how much they paid last time they treated themselves or bought a gift for someone. Products from small businesses tend to be the kind of items that people might buy themselves or others as a gift, and those purchases tend to have a slightly higher price bracket, so it's important to understand that dynamic too.

Remember though that a fact of life for small businesses is that there's always someone who will think your products are overpriced. Be sure to build up a picture from your customer base, not just one isolated piece of feedback.

Many businesses have been derailed with their pricing because one angry customer couldn't believe that they dared to charge those prices. It's happened in pretty much every business I have ever worked in, and I'm certain that there is someone who would walk into a Primark store and find them hideously overpriced.

Consistent feedback from genuine customers that your prices are too high is important information that should be taken into consideration. Random comments from the odd stranger who will probably never buy from you anyway should not. Remember, there's no price low enough for a critic.

Avoid pricing pitfalls

Pay attention to psychological price points such as £10, £20, £50 or £100. For example, it is much better to price at £99 than £102. One is under £100, and one has gone over that psychological barrier.

Avoid "odd" and inconsistent prices. Try and streamline the number of different price points that you use. For example, having items at £12, £13 and £14. Can you just group them together at one price point?

The clearer and easier the price architecture is, the less confusion there will be in the mind of your customer.

The proof of the pudding is in the eating

Ultimately, your customer will dictate your pricing. You can spend many hours theorizing over the best price points, but just set your prices and start selling. You can always adjust prices, although I suggest leaving four to six weeks before changing anything so that you have time to review your sales.

Are you selling very little? Don't assume that this immediately means that your prices are too high, unless you know for a fact that you are considerably more expensive than your immediate competitors (e.g. those of a similar quality to you).

Could your prices actually be too low? Customers make assumptions about your product based on the price, so if you've set the bar too low, they might assume your quality is lacking.

On the flip side, if you are selling an item very quickly (faster than you can get it back into stock, for example) then this is usually a sign that there is room to increase your prices.

The practicalities of raising prices

One of the biggest barriers to people raising their prices is the worry over what people will say. In reality, very few of our customers are so highly attuned to our pricing that they are able to spot immediately if our prices go up. I have worked on three major repricing exercises for national retailers – two where the prices went up, and one where the prices went down.

These were major undertakings, affecting thousands of products across hundreds of stores. How many people noticed or complained? Virtually none.

Some people prefer to let their customers know about a price change. This can be a good way to build trust and communication between you and your customers. In this case, you would inform people that on X date, prices will be increasing, and if they want to purchase beforehand, they'll be able to take advantage of the existing price. This is often a nice way to encourage sales.

If you sell at wholesale, you'd also be able to inform your stockists of your plans and encourage them to purchase from you before the deadline.

Other people prefer to not draw attention to the price increase, and that is equally valid.

Either way, it is often helpful to have some pre-written responses in case you do get a customer complaint. You may never even have to use them, but just knowing that they are there can be enough.

You might want to say:

> *Thank you so much for being a repeat customer, I appreciate your custom. Thank you for your comments regarding the increased price. I recently completed a*

business review and due to rising costs have had to pass on a small portion of the price increase to the customer in order to stay competitive.

I do appreciate that you purchased at a lower price last time. In which case, I would like to offer you a 10% discount on your next order to thank you for your loyalty.

Having this pre-written can be hugely helpful as you go about the task of reviewing and potentially reworking your prices.

When is it not about the margin?

The general rule of thumb is that the bigger the margin, the better, and many businesses would do well to not sell items at all if they are lower margin, rather than tie up their time and efforts on low-margin activities. There are some exceptions to this rule.

Press pieces

In retail terms, it's always good to have what is known as a "shopper stopper". In other words, a really wow piece that is created purely for the purpose of getting attention, both from your customers and potentially PR or press.

These are often the most enjoyable pieces to create for business owners as they allow you to create something that is the fullest expression of your brand or talent. For example, Irene might create a woven tapestry of one of her designs that will look incredible on the wall of her latest photo shoot or at her stand at a trade show, and create a buzz with some of the interior magazines she would love to be featured in.

Emmanuel might create an exclusive vase in collaboration with one of his favourite designers. The pieces may be lower margin as he shares a portion of the sales with the designer, but the interest generated by the collaboration brings new customers to his brand.

These pieces are important for the brand profile, and I highly recommend thinking about what that might look like for your business. They are also one of the rare occasions when the profit margin is not the biggest concern here.

The only caveat is that you should be buying or making very small quantities of these shopper stoppers as they will often be the pieces that create a buzz, but rarely sell at volume. They work best as limited-edition pieces.

High-price items

It would be ideal to make high percentage margins on higher-priced items, but often that is harder to achieve. In that case, you may need to look at the overall cash that you are making on a single sale.

If you sell furniture, and one of your pieces is £600 but with a 30% margin, after VAT, you'll be clearing around £150 on a single sale.

While that is not the best from a margin percentage perspective, you may well decide it is still worthwhile because of the cash amount that you are getting.

Drop shipping

Drop shipping is the process where products are listed for sale on a website, and only physically dispatched from the manufacturer once a sale has taken place. Many businesses use drop shipping to include higher-priced items in their product offering. A baby brand might hold stock of clothing and bedding, but sell nursery furniture via drop shipping where they list a cot on their website and it is sent directly to the customer from the manufacturer.

When you sell drop-shipped items, the likelihood is that you will be getting a smaller percentage of the sale. What that percentage is depends on the agreement with the manufacturer, but may be somewhere between 10% and 30% of the sale price.

Although this is a low margin, the benefit with this model is that you have relatively low risk in having these items on your website. You list them; if they sell, they sell, and if they don't, they don't.

However, a word of caution. While drop shipping sounds like the perfect set-up, it relies on a huge amount of trust with the supplier that you are choosing to drop ship with. You need to make sure that they are keeping you up to date with their availability by item – what happens if you sell something that is out of stock?

You also need to feel confident that they are going to deliver as promised, and that you aren't going to be spending all of your time fielding customer complaints and sorting out disputes over payments. Any drop-shipping agreement needs to be chosen carefully, and you need to be fully aware of what the arrangements will be if the items arrive broken, are lost in transit or if the customer changes their mind.

When you are paying yourself a decent wage

Occasionally, if you are a handmade brand, I come across an issue where the founder has allowed a generous amount of money in the margin calculation to compensate themselves for the time it takes them to make an item.

When that happens, it's sometimes difficult to then, on top of that, hit a high percentage profit margin with that time allowance factored in.

In those circumstances, I am guided by the business owner. If you feel that you are making a decent amount of money for yourself from your activities, then the need to push for a high margin is less urgent.

The reason that most businesses need profit margins in the 60s and 70s to begin with is because otherwise there isn't much left for the owner at the end of it. If you've taken that slice upfront then that is not nearly as big of an issue.

Our case studies

Salma the shop owner

I decided to work through all of the products in my business to see what kind of margins I was getting. Some of them hadn't been updated in a while so it was useful to see where I was at.

For the items that I bought upfront on wholesale, I found that generally those margins were right around the 50% mark. Some other items in the shop had increased over 20% from when I first started buying them, but I hadn't increased any of my prices to reflect that, even though when I checked the manufacturer's RRP had increased.

The other element to factor in is that around 50% of my sales are coming from the sale or return items, which have at most a 25% margin.

This means that, on average, I'm only achieving around a 37.5% in-margin across the whole business. No wonder it feels tight.

I decided to start with a full review of all of my pricing from my wholesale items, making sure that I was, at the very least, using the most up-to-date RRPs.

Next up, I ran through the profit margins on each product, and decided whether or not to keep stocking the ones that were below a 50% margin.

There are three best-selling items that come from the same supplier so I decided to have a conversation with them about the pricing. I was upfront with them, and explained that I was trying to grow my profitability and that I needed to do better with the pricing. I asked them what it would take for me to get these items at £6 instead of the £7.50 I was paying at the moment.

They came back to me with a suggestion that if I spent at least £500 when I placed an order with them, they could offer me a 10% discount. I was happy with that result – although it didn't quite get me where I needed to be, it was a big improvement, and I generally spend nearly £500 on most orders when I do buy from them.

My final task was to make a decision about sale or return items. I looked at what I was selling and approached the top three makers to ask them if they would wholesale me the items instead. One of them absolutely cannot do wholesale pricing, so I'm going to have to keep them as sale or return, but the other two were open to making the switch, especially since it meant that they would be paid upfront.

I also took a look at some of the makers where I hadn't sold anything for a few months, and made arrangements to return their stock. This was probably the hardest part – I hated giving people the news, but most of them were fine with it. One of the artists was actually hugely relieved as they are about to do a fair and will be able to take what I returned to them to add to their offering.

Removing the unproductive sale or return stock from the shelf has helped me feel more in control and positive about the products on the shelves. I've also had a few nice comments from customers about the shop feeling airy and easy to browse in.

Emmanuel the e-commerce seller

I decided that I had to stop sticking my head in the sand and recalculate the margins after VAT registration. I was a bit nervous, but to be honest, I'd forgotten that I can now deduct the VAT from the prices I was paying on a few items, so that helped soften the blow.

Looking at these items, including the new fees from the fulfilment centre, it did show me that there were a couple where the percentage margin had dropped. One or two of these products were slow to sell anyway, so I decided to discontinue them.

One of them, a minimalist coffee table, is only a 30% margin once I factor in the cost of shipping and the storage fees at the fulfilment centre. However, given that I make £100 on every sale, I decided to keep this in the range as it provides a nice cash injection when it does sell.

Irene the illustrator

As I suspected, when I looked at my numbers, I was happy with where they were.

It was a useful exercise though to be thinking about my margins, because it helped me assess my ceramics samples that I've been developing.

I used the pricing review strategy to work out what I would need to charge for the items that I want to sell, compared to three other businesses who sell ceramics made in the same way. I reverse engineered what I'd need to be paying the manufacturer for these items and it was way off.

I spoke to my contact at the factory and asked them what it would take for me to get the price that I wanted. They laughed and said that this wasn't workable unless I was ordering over 10,000 per style, which is just completely unrealistic for me at the moment for an untested product. As frustrating as that was to hear, it also helped me make the decision quickly about what I wanted to do, and I decided to pause the development on the ceramics for now.

Conclusion

Think of your in-margin as the foundation that your whole business is built on. If you don't get this right, you will find that what you are building is shaky.

It's worth spending the time to check your numbers. Even if you feel like you are starting with your in-margin much lower than you would like, it's still worth putting in the effort to check your numbers and start monitoring from where you are right now.

Once you have thoroughly checked and examined your in-margin, it's time to consider the next element of your profit margin – the bottom teeth, also known as your out-margin.

Key points

- The best way to keep an eye on your margins is to check the margin on every item before you commit to purchasing it, factoring in every cost.
- You should also be checking your margins every time you get a new invoice to make sure that you are totally on top of any price increases.

- Be aware of any items that are below your ideal margin, and think about whether or not you want to continue to sell them.
- Consider other ways that you could bring the margin in on target, whether that's changing suppliers, negotiating or reverse engineering the product to fit your margin goals.
- Repricing your products is a last resort, but if you need to review your pricing, make sure you do it in a logical way.
- There are some cases where margin percentage is not as important, but these are the exception rather than the rule.
- You can get your free margin calculator at www.resilientretailclub.com/tigertoolkit and details of more help in the 'Additional resources' section at the end of the book.

Over to you

1. Have you checked your profit margins recently? Go to www.resilientretailclub.com/tigertoolkit and download the Tiger Tamer's Toolkit. Get the margin calculator and run through as many of your products as you can.

2. Identify your worst-margin items. Looking at the list of potential options, what can you do to improve them?

3. If you have a lot of items that are below your target margin, focus on your best sellers. If you start with your best-selling items and look to improve your profit margin there, it will have the biggest impact.

4. How can you make sure that you are regularly checking your margins and screening new items as well going forward?

5. Are you happy with your prices? Have you reviewed them, including your competitors, in the last few months?

6. Take some time to review your prices and decide if there are any that could be tweaked up to improve your overall in-margin.

CHAPTER 4

THE BITE – THE BOTTOM TEETH

Now that we've had the opportunity to thoroughly investigate the impact of the product costs on the profitability of your business, we're going to look in more detail at the other factors impacting how much money you are making when you sell your products.

As well as measuring your in-margin (the top teeth) with all the costs associated with it, you also need to look at the **actual** margin you sell your products for (the bottom teeth). This figure is known as the out-margin. If the in-margin represents how much money you would sell an item for if you sold it at full price, which is looking forward into the future, the out-margin is an analysis of historical sales data to show what actually happened.

Another way of thinking about it is that your in-margin is based on looking at each product in your business individually, with the out-margin focusing instead on a blended number that looks across all of the sales for a particular time period. The in-margin is theoretical; the out-margin is historical.

Why do we start with the in-margin? The in-margin sets the foundation for profitability in a business. Without the in-margin being at the right level, the bite is too big and you'll struggle to make the business profitable.

To be a tiger tamer, you need to look at both. You absolutely have to have your in-margin at the right place before looking at your out-margin as otherwise you won't know whether or not your problems with profitability are coming from a low in-margin or other issues in the business.

As a reminder of how to tell the difference between in-margin and out-margin, when a product is purchased by you, it is coming **in** to your business. The price that you pay for this item compared to what you are planning on selling it for is your **in-margin**.

When a product is sold by you to a customer, it's going **out** of the business. The difference between what you paid for this product and what you actually sold it for is your **out-margin**.

Let's look at an example of an in-margin and out-margin.

Emmanuel has a set of stainless-steel tumblers that retail for £12 each. The cost of the product and all associated costs is £3.

If you remember from Chapter 3, the in-margin is as follows:

In-margin (20% VAT-registered businesses) = ((selling price/1.2) − total product costs)/(selling price/1.2) × 100

The in-margin, therefore, is ((£12/1.2) − £3)/(£12/1.2) × 100 = (£10 − £3)/£10 × 100 = £7/£10 × 100 = 70%

When Emmanuel sells these tumblers, they are typically bought as part of a multibuy offer that he is running on his website. Buy three, get one free.

Therefore, when he analyses his sales data, he finds that in the previous month he sold eight tumblers, generating £72 in sales, as two were free.

Since he sold them at a multibuy discount, which works out at £9 each, clearly he was not going to make the in-margin that he had calculated at £12 retail. Therefore, he needs to run his actual sales compared to his product costs, and that is the out-margin.

When it comes to taming the tiger it's important to understand not just what you **could** make on a product, but what you are **actually** making.

For more support, go to www.resilientretailclub.com/tigertoolkit to get the free resources to help you with some of the concepts and formulas in this chapter.

Our case studies

Salma the shop owner

This is a problem area for me, especially when it comes to selling online. If someone orders using a 10% introductory discount, and I've had to include the cost of postage and packaging too, sometimes I'm barely making any profit.

I even used to sell the sale or return products online, the ones that I make 25% commission on, but thankfully I saw sense and stopped because I was literally making pennies.

In the shop, I don't do much in the way of discounting, so that doesn't seem to be a big problem. However, there is one product that seems to be skewing my figures. I sell a little badge and patch with the name of our town under a rainbow and it's incredibly popular. I sell more of this product than anything else, and it's only £2 for the badge or £3 for the patch, at a 30% margin – plus I make a donation to the local charity of £1 for every sale. Some weeks this one product skews my overall figures.

Emmanuel the e-commerce seller

As soon as I read about the bottom teeth, I knew that this was going to be one of the areas that is tricky for me in my business. Even though I start at around a 50% margin on most things and higher on my own products, I already know that a lot of my products are bought by my customers with a discount.

My website has a 15% off code for anyone who joins the mailing list, and while this seems like it's working to help me get email addresses, I know that nearly every order is using this code. On top of that, if sales are slow, sometimes I panic and do a 25% off code for payday because I want to hit my sales target that month.

I also don't limit my codes in any way; it's just money off everything. So, if someone is buying a bundle on the tumblers and getting 25% off, even though they start with a decent margin I end up making so little money that it makes me feel a little sick.

I was looking back at my social media and I realized that I did a code at the end of four out of the last five months. The majority of my sales are made using some kind of discount.

Irene the illustrator

I was intrigued to hear about the out-margin idea because it feels like a piece of the puzzle that's been missing before.

I think for me what will be affecting the out-margin for the whole business is the fact that I sell so much at wholesale, which has a much lower margin.

I was all smug about my in-margins being so high, but in reality a large proportion of my sales are coming via wholesale, so that the actual out-margin is much lower than I would like to imagine. It's a good way of checking the business.

How do you calculate the out-margin?

The out-margin is calculated by looking at the sales value that you took in a month and taking away the cost of those sales.

Out-margin (non-VAT-registered businesses) = (total sales – total product costs including packaging – selling fees – postage)/total sales × 100

Out-margin (20% VAT-registered businesses) = ((total sales/1.2) – total product costs including packaging – selling fees – postage)/(total sales/1.2) × 100

Let's say Salma's monthly sales are £15,000.

Total sales inc VAT and postage	£15,000
Net sales ex VAT	£12,500
VAT	£2,500
Payment fees	£450
Postage (for online)	£600
Cost of goods sold including packaging	£7,450
Profit	£4,000
Out-margin	32%

Out-margin (20% VAT-businesses) = ((total sales/1.2)
– total product costs including packaging
– selling fees – postage)/(total sales/1.2) × 100

= ((£15,000/1.2) – £7,450 – £450 – £600)/(£15,000/1.2) × 100
= (£12,500 – £8,500)/(£12,500) × 100
= £4,000 £4,000/£12,500 × 100 = 32%

Postage and packaging

You may notice that when we calculated the in-margin, for every item we broke down how much money was remaining after tax, postage, packaging and so on. This was because it was a good check on how much money was left in each individual case, and to help identify the products that were not profitable or where postage was prohibitively expensive compared to the profit generated from the product.

However, for the out-margin, when we refer to the product costs, typically this is calculated using the cost from the supplier (plus any fees or shipping costs that it took to get the products to you), as well as the cost of the packaging that you would typically use to ship it out or sell in the shop.

This is because it is hard to estimate otherwise how much you will have spent in that month on packaging. You may be able to see how much you paid the packaging company in any given month, but this can be misleading if you were stocking up for future months.

Postage, however, is usually an easy number to get hold of as you will be able to track how much you paid your courier or Royal Mail in a particular month. By separating the postage out into a separate line when you look at your out-margin, you will be able to have a more accurate picture of how much it is costing you.

For some people, if their accountancy software is correctly set up and syncing to their sales, the cost of goods sold will be automatically calculated so that each month you can easily see your sales and the product costs associated with those sales.

However, despite this being the best-case scenario, I would say that this is not the reality for many of the businesses I work with. You may find that the best use of your time, to enable you to get a good understanding of what your out-margin is, is to talk to your accountant about how you can set up your accountancy software to input all of your product costs and get an accurate figure for the cost of goods sold from your monthly accounts data.

If, for any reason, it's not an option to set up your accountancy software to correctly pull through your cost of goods sold, it can be manually calculated using your sales data and something that I refer to as "the master list".

Calculating your out-margin does require some basic spreadsheet work, as well as setting up a couple of templates to help you. It will require some work but is definitely worth it. It's so powerful because it gives you clarity on not just your theoretical margins, but on how much you are actually making when you are selling.

For many people, it is the missing piece of the puzzle, without which they cannot understand why their business is not as profitable as they would like it to be. Once you know what your out-margin is, you will have a much deeper understanding of your business.

The master list

What is a master list? It's something that will be very useful as you grow your business and focus on the numbers driving your profitability.

Modern e-commerce websites are fantastic from a usability point of view, making it easy to quickly upload many products. However, in my experience, they are not set up with anything more than the most basic analysis in mind.

It's tempting to think that because you can easily see a list of your products on your website platform, you do not need to maintain a separate list in a spreadsheet. But having this list as your central reference point can help you in so many ways when it comes to better analysing and understanding your business.

The master list is also sometimes referred to as a range plan. It is a record, in a spreadsheet, of every item that you sell, along with some key information about each one. Some of the elements that you should include are:

- A unique identifying code – this is important as having a unique identifier makes analysis so much easier, as I will explain later. You don't need anything special to create these codes – you could start with number 1 as your first product and move on sequentially from there.
- The item description such as "Graphic Tee – Daisy Print".
- Details about the variants – for example, colour or size. You may want to have both colour and size, especially if you sell clothing.
- The cost price from the supplier, preferably including the costs associated with getting the product to you, for example the shipping and duty costs.
- The cost of packaging used to typically send an item out to customers or sell in the shop.
- The retail price.
- The in-margin – this can be a calculation.
- The category of product – for example, "ladies T-shirt" (we'll talk more about categories in the next chapter).

- The name of the supplier.
- The status of the product – this is useful to know. Is the product current or discontinued? In other words, if you sold out, would you reorder it or not? This sounds like simple information, but it can be hugely beneficial if you review and keep this column updated as you go along. As your business grows, you will have team members handling customer queries, for example, and being able to see whether or not an item is discontinued will help them give accurate information to customers without having to ask you first.

Other elements that may or may not be relevant for your business:

- The seasonality of the product – typically more relevant for clothing companies; it is very useful to know if it's a Spring/Summer or Autumn/Winter product, or perhaps a seasonless basic.
- The occasion it belongs to, for example, Easter, Christmas, Mother's Day or None – particularly useful for cards, gift wrap or gifting and themed items.
- Any other category and subcategory that is relevant to your business. For example, if you run a candle business, you might want to know which fragrance an item is, especially if you use it across multiple products. Later on, this will allow you to analyse which fragrance sells the most. If you're not sure about how to structure this for your business, we'll be talking about this later.

This master list forms the basis of all the analysis that you will need going forward, and should be kept updated as you add new products. By making this accurate and keeping it updated, you will be able to run many types of analysis on your sales and stock that will help you make better decisions about the care and keeping of your tiger.

Want some help creating your master list? You can find a checklist of what to include at www.resilientretailclub.com/tigertoolkit

Details of more support can also be found in the 'Additional resources' section at the end of this book.

Calculating out-margin using the master list

Now that you have a list of all of your products, how do you work out your out-margin from the master list? For this you will need to get the previous month's sales split out by product, including the quantity and sales value.

Most platforms will allow you to download a list of your sales for the previous month, literally a list of every order, which you can get in the form of a .csv file. CSV (which stands for comma separated variables) files are text files and can be pasted into a spreadsheet and manipulated into data.

At this point, depending on how you feel about spreadsheets, you may be thinking that you are never, ever going to start messing around with data and text files and you may as well stop now.

I can tell you that I have worked with many different people over the years, and if you take it slow, it's all extremely logical. If you can learn to work with this data, you will have powerful ways of looking at your business.

If you absolutely, positively, cannot engage with these numbers, I suggest that you find someone in your life who will help you. However, before you decide that you definitely cannot do it yourself, I would urge you to spend just a few minutes giving it a go. It might be easier than you think.

What about a system that does all this?

One of the biggest questions that I ask myself about this type of exercise is whether or not it's the right thing to even try to show people how to run this analysis themselves, or whether I should instead be encouraging them to use a reporting or stock analysis system which will do these calculations for them.

The absolute ideal situation would be to set up a system that would allow you to look at all of your sales data in this way. There are systems that will do this, but in my experience most are expensive for small businesses, and even if they do part of the analysis well, they don't always show the full picture.

So, on balance, I'd say that the time it would take you to set up and learn one of these systems, as well as the cost, makes them a less attractive option.

A spreadsheet is quick to set up and, in my opinion, will not only cost you nothing but will also teach you skills that will come in useful.

Vlookup

What is a Vlookup? This formula is probably one of the most useful tricks when it comes to data analysis. While it looks quite daunting, it essentially allows you to match up data in two different places. It is the key to much of the analysis needed to understand your business better. Being able to pull different lists of data together into one sheet means you can combine your sales data with your cost price data, or your stock data with your sales data – the applications are endless.

I like to think of a Vlookup as looking something up in an old-style telephone directory. You just need to tell the spreadsheet what you want to look up and where the information is kept.

This formula works the same whether you are using Excel or the free spreadsheet tool, Google Sheets. Its magic lies in allowing you to combine two lists of data, and it doesn't matter if the data isn't in the same order in each list.

Running a Vlookup requires a unique identifier that unites the data from one sheet with that of another. So, if you want to run sales data out of your website and pull in information from your master list, you'll need a unique identifier to help you do so.

Let's imagine that you want to calculate your out-margin. You have two tabs in a spreadsheet with two sets of information in them.

One tab contains information about your sales from the previous month that you pasted in from a CSV file and looks like this:

	A	B	C	D	E
1	Item number	Item description	Quantity sold	Sales value	Item cost
2	12345	Greetings card – Birthday Rainbow	5	£16	
3	12346	Ladies Hoodie Heart Print	2	£90	
4	12697	Postcard – Seafront	5	£4.50	

One tab is called Master List, and the first few columns look like this:

	A	B	C	D	E	F	G	H
1	Item number	Item description	Colour	Supplier	Product category	Sub-category	Retail price	Cost price
2	12345	Greetings card – Birthday Rainbow	n.a.	Greetings Cards R Us	Cards	Birthday	£3.50	£1.25
3	12346	Ladies Hoodie Heart Print	Pink	Sweat-shirts Ltd	Ladies Fashion	Sweat-shirts	£50	£20
4	12697	Postcard – Seafront	n.a.	Greetings Cards R Us	Cards	Post-cards	£1	£0.40

Let's assume that we want to use a Vlookup formula in the first tab in column E to work out what the item costs.

The formula you need to type into cell E2 looks like this:

```
=VLOOKUP(A2,Master List !A:H,8,false)
```

Let's take it step by step.

Firstly, most formulas in spreadsheets start with =, followed by the name of the formula. By typing

=VLOOKUP(

you are informing the spreadsheet that you want to use a Vlookup formula.

Next

=VLOOKUP(A2

This tells the spreadsheet that the item you want to look up is in cell A2. Usually this would be the unique identifier of the product that you are looking up data for.

=VLOOKUP(A2,Master List !A:H

Now you are indicating where the data is that you want to look up. The code you are looking for must be in the first column of the data you want to use. Then you just need to include as many columns as you need so that the data you want to bring back is included. In this case, we need to include all the columns from A to H because the data we want, the cost price, is in column H.

=VLOOKUP(A2,Master List !A:H,8

The number, in this case, 8, represents the number of columns you want the spreadsheet to count over to find the data to bring back. If the unique identifier is in the first column, and the cost price is in the eighth column, then you want it to count over eight columns (the first column is 1, second is 2 etc.).

=VLOOKUP(A2,Master List !A:H,8,false)

False at the end of the formula means that you only want to bring back the exact match. If you select true, then it will return the closest match to the unique identifier.

If you'd prefer to watch an explainer video for a Vlookup, visit www.resilientretailclub.com/tigertoolkit for a bonus video to walk you through the formula.

Using the data to calculate the out-margin

Let's say you set up your spreadsheets as above, with one of them showing your sales data for the month. You need to pull into the sales spreadsheet the cost price for each product, and then add another column, F in the example below, to multiply the cost price by the number that you sold.

	A	B	C	D	E	F
1	Item number	Item description	Quantity sold	Sales value	Item cost	Total cost value
2	12345	Greetings card – Birthday Rainbow	5	£16.00	£1.25	£6.25
3	12346	Ladies Hoodie Heart Print	2	£90.00	£20.00	£40.00
4	12697	Postcard – Seafront	5	£4.50	£0.40	£2.00
	Total			£110.50		£48.25

You can now use the following formulas to calculate the out-margin.

Out-margin (non-VAT-registered businesses) = (total sales – total product costs including packaging – selling fees – postage)/total sales × 100

Out-margin (20% VAT-registered businesses) = ((total sales/1.2) – total product costs including packaging – selling fees –postage)/(total sales/1.2) × 100

You'll be able to pull the total sales and the total product costs from the spreadsheet above.

Once you have run this data for every sale then you will be in a position to summarize the data and identify what your actual out-margin is.

Let's imagine in the example above that the selling fees were 3% of the sales and the postage costs were £10.

Assuming that the business was not VAT registered, calculating the out-margin would look like this:

Out-margin (non-VAT-registered businesses) =
(total sales – total product costs including packaging –
selling fees – postage)/total sales × 100

$$= (£110.50 - £48.25 - (£110.50 * 3\%) - £10)/£110.50 \times 100$$
$$= (£110.50 - £48.25 - £3.31 - £10)/£110.50 \times 100$$
$$= £48.94/£110.5 \times 100 = 44.3\%$$

What can impact your out-margin?

Once you have run your out-margin calculation, you may notice that it is always lower than the average in-margin that you identified when looking at your products one by one, as we discussed in the previous chapter.

For example, let's say Irene the illustrator has run through all of her in-margins and feels good about them. She knows that on her paper goods, in particular, she is making well above 70%.

After doing that exercise, she feels both pleased and also confused. She is certain that her profits at the end of each month are not nearly that high.

She downloads all of her sales data for a previous month and analyses how much profit she made on her sales. She can see that it averages out at around 60%. How does she manage to go from over 70% to 60%?

This difference between your in-margin and out-margin is often very confusing for product businesses. However, the good news is that this gap is definitely within your control. While your in-margin is subject to change based on anything from rising prices to currency fluctuations, your out-margin is largely affected by decisions that you make in your business.

Some things that impact your out-margin are postage, discounts, reductions, mix of products and your sales channels.

Postage

Look at how much you are charging customers for postage compared to how much that postage is costing you. It could be having a significant impact on your profits. It's not unusual for businesses that I work with to be spending around 10% of their turnover on postage.

Make sure that offering free postage makes sense for your business. If you are finding that overall your profit margins are low, you may want to revisit your postage costs.

The reason that free postage is pushed by platforms such as Etsy or NotOnTheHighStreet.com is because studies have shown that people are more likely to buy if there is free postage. A customer would rather pay £28 with free shipping than £25 with £3 shipping. There are definitely reasons to offer free postage, but it's important to understand what that is doing to your margins.

Would it be better, for example, to look at offering free shipping only above a certain spending limit?

Discounts

This is one of the most significant impacts on your profit margins. What discounts are your customers using?

Introductory discounts

Businesses often use introductory discounts to entice customers to join their email lists. While this is an effective way to get email addresses, you have to ask yourself whether your margins can support this tactic. For example, if you are already selling products from other businesses and therefore your product margins are already lower than expected, plus your shipping is eating into your profits, then adding a discount on top of all of these costs may not be the right approach.

Promotional discounts

Promotional discounts are offers that you make to your customers – for example, 20% off everything or selected discounts on certain products. Although these discounts can be good for driving sales, they are hard on your profit margins.

My mantra with promotions is "they look like they are for the customer, but they are actually for you". Promotions need to work for your business. If you run a 20% off discount twice a year and that brings in vital revenue at key times, then that promotion is working for you. It's a short-term discount, it will impact your profit margin but should drive more sales to compensate.

If you run repeated offers giving the customer a blanket discount (money off everything, perhaps using a code or automatically set up on your website), then a few things may start to happen. Firstly, the customer is going to become accustomed to purchasing from you at a discount and will start waiting for the next offer. We all have brands that we know are not worth purchasing from at full price as an offer will be along soon. You don't want your customers to think of your business that way.

Once you have that reputation, it's incredibly hard to reverse that perception. It takes a long time before the customer stops holding out for a discount, which can be a seriously nail-biting time for your business. It is far better to never get that reputation to begin with.

The other thing that happens is that the offers will become less effective over time. The more you run a blanket discount, the less interest you will generate each time.

> Think of discounts like spices. A little creates interest and excitement, and too much ruins the dish.

Use them to selectively season your business, not constantly as a way of driving sales.

Finally, the other impact of a blanket discount is that it will heavily impact your profit margins over time. Your customer will simply buy what they were going to buy anyway, but at 20% off. Your best sellers will still be your best sellers but your customers will buy them at a lower price than you might otherwise have been able to command for them.

Blanket discounts are brand damaging when used too much. They damage both your reputation as a quality business and also your ability to command the kind of prices needed to achieve a decent margin.

Targeted discounts are better than blanket discounts. By those, I mean something like "selected lines 20% off" or "30% off all candles". In this category, I might also include discounts sent to a very targeted group with a specific reason. For example, a 10% discount that is sent via email to anyone who has purchased from you but not in the last six months, in order to incentivize a repeat purchase.

The reason these are better is because they are more controlled. You are using them to shape and mould customer behaviour, and to guide them to do something that you'd like them to do.

For example, if you have a product area that is slow moving (we'll talk more about stock management in later chapters), then a discount to help clear stock would be appropriate. The same goes for a stock clearance sale where you are choosing to discount items heavily to liquidate stock and improve your cash flow.

The key with all types of discounts is to closely monitor what percentage of your sales comes from full-price sales and what percentage comes from discounted sales.

You should aim for a full-price sale, where the customer is paying the exact price that you intended for that product. If you make full-price sales your goal, your out-margin will be closer to your average in-margin. The larger the percentage of discounted sales, the lower your out-margin will be.

Topline sales are great, and seeing your revenue grow each time is very motivating. Just watch that you aren't growing your revenue purely by discounting.

I was once employed by a seven-figure business, where I was brought in to analyse their profitability and discovered that 80–90% of all of their sales in one product area were coming either from old-season clearance stock or off the back of a discount offer.

It was quite shocking to see how low their full price, non-promoted sales were. The issue was that a lot of these products were bought in from other businesses, so as a result we were making a margin of less than 50% to start with. Taking a further 20%, or sometimes even 30%, off on a regular basis was just too much to bear. This story didn't end well – the business was loss-making when I joined and eventually collapsed.

It wasn't quite as black and white as saying that the discounting caused the collapse, but it was a factor. It also hid the fact that the business was not growing their sales in a profitable way, but instead relying on discounting to grow.

I know that this is all sounding very doom and gloom, but the truth is you need to be aware at the very least what sort of an impact your discounting strategy is having on your profit margins.

It is not uncommon for us to discover, when working with a client, that the cause of feeling that there "isn't enough money in the business" is coming from a combination of the in-margin being too low and then excessive discounting or other offers making the out-margin wafer thin.

I would say the majority of tiger businesses I see have problems because of the bite, so it's well worth your time to investigate what is going on for your business.

Other factors affecting your out-margin

As well as the actions that you are taking in your business, such as using discounts, other elements impact your out-margin that are worth taking into consideration.

1. Seasonality

Depending on your business, you may find that your out-margin fluctuates throughout the year. Certainly you will find that during sale periods it will be lower due to a higher proportion of discounted sales compared to full-price sales.

You may also find that at certain times, for example if you typically sell Christmas gift sets at a higher retail price, your out-margin is doing particularly well. It's definitely an interesting statistic to look at on a monthly basis.

2. Sales channels

Out-margin is something that will fluctuate considerably between your sales channels, so it's very useful to understand what it looks like for each of your sales platforms.

This information helps you to make decisions about where to focus your time and energy as a business owner. It's also important to understand where to allocate your stock if you have limited quantities and lots of places you could sell it.

The simplest way to get this information is to run your out-margin calculation for each different platform, and understand what your total sales and cost of goods sold are for each one. Different platforms take differing amounts of commission from businesses, so it's useful to compare your margins across them.

It will also help you to keep things separate if you have a business that sells at both retail and wholesale. Wholesale channels have much lower margins than retail channels, and it is very useful to understand these dynamics. With wholesale you are most likely going to be pursuing that strategy with certain goals in mind. Growing your brand awareness, evening out your cash flow and boosting the quantities you can order from your manufacturer are three great reasons to have a wholesale business that are not related to the profit margin.

So, even if you identify that one of your sales channels is below the others, it doesn't mean that you can't choose to sell on them. However, it will help you to understand what is happening in your business and make improvements.

It can also help you make decisions about which products you want to sell on which platforms. One of the mistakes that I often see people make is when they feel like they have to sell every item on every platform. Not only is this not practical, but many businesses will have items that are lower margin than others and cannot therefore be sold at wholesale, for example due to the much lower margins.

It can work to your benefit to have products that can only be found on your website and nowhere else. It gives people a reason to visit your site – as they will know that you have the biggest range. So don't be afraid to be selective about which products sell on which sales channels.

3. Mix of product

One thing that often catches businesses out when they are looking at their out-margin is the impact that certain products doing well can have on the margin. Ironically, we think that what we want more than anything in our business is for sales to grow. However, we do need to be aware of WHAT it is that is selling and how that is going to impact our overall out-margin.

Let's look at Salma's situation. She's noticed that one product in particular can sometimes impact her profits. It's a low-price badge with a rainbow that says "proud resident" of her seaside town. The product has a low margin, but it's so popular that she features it heavily in all of her marketing.

When Salma runs her margin analysis, she is surprised to see that her overall margin percentage has dropped. Digging in further, she realizes that 30% of her sales in the last month were coming from this badge. While this meant she had sold an impressive number, she had inadvertently brought down her margin.

This was not necessarily the wrong decision – after all, we can assume that these customers were coming in, purchasing the badge and, in some cases at least, purchasing something else as well. It's fine if this is what happens, but the most important thing is that Salma is aware instead of suddenly realizing months later that this is an issue.

She could also make a decision to increase the price on that badge since it was doing so well and help nudge up her overall profits. Or maybe it's time to go back to the manufacturer and ask for a better price since she has ordered so many.

How do you improve your out-margin?

Let's say that you have run your analysis and realize that there is an issue with your out-margin. What steps do you need to take to improve this?

The first step, as with most things in your business, is to gain an understanding of why your out-margin is lower than you would like it to be.

For example, is it because your in-margin is too low? That would be the first port of call for many business owners as it follows that a low in-margin will cause a low out-margin.

However, let's say that you have worked your way through the previous chapter on in-margin and are satisfied with where you are, what now?

The next most logical step is to take a look at the percentage of your sales coming from promotions, as compared to full-price sales.

Depending on which platform you are using to sell, you may be able to get a report on how many sales have come from discounts, or perhaps the total value of the discounts that have been applied to your business overall.

If you believe that this is a major issue behind your lower than desired out-margin, you can start looking at ways to reduce the amount of sales that happen with a discount.

- You could look at any introductory offers that are being used regularly – do you need to make them applicable only over a certain amount or play around with other offers?
- Are your free-postage discounts set at the right levels? For example, are they around 10% higher than your average order value to encourage customers to spend more?
- How often are you running promotions that use a discount? Is this the right level? Could you re-plan your marketing to keep you focused on a variety of activities as opposed to a discount?
- Can you make sure that any discounts are aimed at shaping customer behaviour and keep blanket discounts (money off everything) to an absolute minimum?
- Is your product mix skewing your out-margin? Are you focusing too heavily on promoting items that are not as high margin?
- Can you put these items into a bundle offer with other higher-priced items to allow you to sell those?

The crucial element of managing your out-margin is tracking it. Make sure you check your out-margin once a month, and see what difference the actions that you are taking are making to your business.

Our case studies

Salma the shop owner

I decided to look at my numbers in more detail. I have identified that profit margin is something that I struggle with due to the low-margin items that I am stocking as well as too much stock being sold through clearance and at discount.

After reviewing my assortment, working to improve the margins of the products I sell, as well as looking at other alternatives to discounts, I was delighted to see that I managed to move my out-margin to 43% from 32%.

What made me feel even more happy was when I ran my profit and loss before and after the switch. With nothing else changing, I have gone from running a loss each month to showing a profit. That is the power of your margin. It can change a loss-making business into a profitable one without your sales changing at all.

	Before	After
Gross sales inc VAT	£15,000	£15,000
Net sales ex VAT	£12,500	£12,500
Payment fees	£450	£450
Postage (for online)	£600	£600
Cost of goods sold	£7,450	£6,075
Profit	£4,000	£5,375
Out-margin	32%	43%
Rent/rates/utilities	£1,500	£1,500
Staffing	£2,500	£2,500
Misc other costs	£300	£300
Net profit	£-300	£1,075

Emmanuel the e-commerce seller

This exercise showed me that I needed to do something to stop the discounting. It was hard at first. I switched off the welcome discount and it felt like people stopped signing up overnight.

Over the next three months, I decided to try three different lead magnets (the name given to something you give away in return for email sign-ups) to see if I could persuade customers to join the email list without a discount. In the end, I found that a simple PDF with a round-up of my top "design on a budget" tips was the best at driving email sign-ups.

The promotional sales were tougher. I decided that I was going to stop running the end-of-month discount, and that first month it was very nerve-wracking.

However, I decided to look at my profit and I was amazed to find that it wasn't as different as you might think. Not only that, because I hadn't had that rush of additional orders at the end of the month, I hadn't needed to pay a big fulfilment fee so the whole thing felt smoother and easier.

Because I wasn't generating these big topline sales, I wasn't nearly as busy with customer service queries either, and I didn't have to place a big top-up order. It felt like it was more manageable.

Irene the illustrator

As suspected, when I looked at my out-margin, I could see that, in reality, it's closer to 60% rather than well over 70% that I got when I ran my in-margin. This is down to my wholesale margin being so much lower, and wholesale being such a big part of my business.

I still felt that 60% was a pretty good place to be and I liked seeing the actual number instead of just having this vague idea that it was probably lower than I thought it was. I am going to keep tracking this every month to keep an eye on it.

Conclusion

This is truly one area of the business where knowledge is power. In return for some time investment in setting up templates, you'll have an opportunity to understand how profitable your sales truly are.

Make sure you look at your out-margin – at the absolute minimum once a quarter, although once a month would be best. Make sure that you are also checking your discounted sales to get a clear picture of the impact that these are having.

Once you have mastered the tiger's bite, you will have made great progress towards understanding and taming your tiger. However, there's more to be done, and the next step is all about managing that tiger's tail!

Key points

- While the in-margin underpins how much money you could theoretically be making, the out-margin is a measure of the money you are actually making.
- Your out-margin is always going to be lower than your in-margin because it's the bottom teeth in the bite. The top teeth take the first bite and the bottom teeth take off the rest. You need to start with a decent in-margin to help your out-margin stay at a decent level.
- In-margin and out-margins are key metrics to monitor in your business, because if you focus on continuing to improve them, then you'll be growing your sales profitably.
- If your out-margin is lower than you want it to be, first check if that's because your in-margin is too low.
- Once you've established that it's related to your out-margin, look at discounting, over-use of offers, product mix and so on.

- Visit www.resilientretailclub.com/tigertoolkit for a checklist for your master list, as well as a Vlookup explainer video.
- Details of additional support can be found in the 'Additional resources' section at the end of the book.

Over to you

1. Using any reporting you might have, your accounting system or by creating your own master list, look at your cost of goods sold for the last month and calculate your out-margin.

2. Look at your best-selling products – are there any that are skewing your out-margin?

3. What current discounts are being used in your business? Are they all strictly necessary? Where can you reduce their use?

4. Look at your promotional calendar – to what extent are you using blanket discounts? Can you look at alternatives?

CHAPTER 5

UNDERSTANDING THE SIZE OF YOUR TIGER'S TAIL

There are two key fundamental principles that govern product businesses. The first, that we have explored in great depth in Chapters 3 and 4, is that you cannot grow a profitable product business unless you make enough money every time you make a sale.

The other fundamental principle is that the faster that you are paid by the customer for your products, the better your cash flow will be and the more profitable your business will become.

If you buy stock and sell it immediately, you are able to then reinvest that cash into your business. However, if you buy stock and then only a small portion of it sells, then the remainder becomes trapped cash. There is less in your bank account to reinvest in new products or more of your best sellers, and eventually your cash flow will slow to a trickle.

One of the biggest indicators of whether or not a business feels cash rich or cash poor is how quickly stock turns.

In this chapter, and in Chapter 6, we're going to look at how you can identify areas of unproductive stock to help free up that trapped cash and improve your profitability. To do that, we're going to start with the tail.

The bigger the tail, the bigger the tiger

One of the most challenging aspects of running a product business is, well, the products themselves. Stock is cash that is tied up in your business. Look around you, and instead of seeing your stock as physical items, imagine that they are money instead.

If the item sells for £10, imagine that it is a £10 note sitting there. When you start to look at your stock this way, it becomes obvious where the money in your business is. If you have nothing in your bank account but have a warehouse full of stock, this is your answer to the question of why your cash flow is so stressful.

Within your stock, however, not all of it is created equal. Product businesses are very often governed by the 80/20 rule, also known as the Pareto principle.

For those who are not familiar with the Pareto principle, Pareto was an Italian economist who identified that 80% of results came from just 20% of actions. In a retail business what this equates to is that 80% of your sales are likely to be coming from 20% of your range. If you have 100 items in your range, the likelihood is that 80% of your sales will be coming from your top 20.

I have run this analysis for many different businesses of different sizes. I have looked at businesses that had thousands of products and businesses that had a handful. I have found that the 80/20 rule applies to the majority of product businesses. Even if it's not quite 80/20, the likelihood is, at the very most, that 20-40% of your stock is generating 80% of your sales.

There are always, in every business that I have worked in or with, the best sellers that outperform everything else. These are your stars – the items that are profitable, revenue driving and customer capturing. It is useful to know what these are in your business because it gives you insight into what is creating sales and moving you forward.

Much of success in retail can be boiled down to "do more of what works, and less of what doesn't" – in this case, if you know what your best 20% of products look like, you can build and develop these to help grow your sales.

However, the flip side is that 20% of your sales are likely to be coming from the remaining 80% of your range. This stock is generally much less productive than the stock of your best sellers. The name of the game in a product business is to reduce the amount of stock that you are holding in this unproductive 80%. These products are referred to, in the businesses that I worked in throughout my career, as "the tail". And the bigger the tail, or the more stock that you hold in those unproductive products, the bigger the tiger. That is to say, the more likely it is that your business feels like it's unprofitable, the worse the cash flow and the more unwieldy the whole business becomes.

This is where your spare cash goes. This is why you feel like as soon as money comes in, it has to go out again to cover expenses. Carrying too much stock in that tail is a major risk and will stop you from building a profitable business.

In this chapter, we're going to examine how to identify your tail and what to do about it. Go to www.resilientretailclub. com/tigertoolkit to get the free resources to help you with the concepts in this chapter.

Our case studies

Salma the shop owner

We definitely have a tail! In my case, unsold seasonal stock is a problem that's been growing steadily worse since we opened six years ago. Every year, after Christmas is over, I put the unsold stock into the stock room. Well, "stock room" makes it sound a lot grander than it is; it's more like a walk-in stock cupboard round the back sandwiched between the staff loo and the back door.

To begin with, it was a small amount and it was fine. Then the next year, I took out the same box and put two boxes back after Christmas. Fast forward to now, and I can't use the stock room anymore. When we get deliveries, they have to go straight out on the shop floor. I have a nasty suspicion that some of the boxes in the stockroom have got damp as there was a leaking pipe in the bathroom last year and we were never able to get all the way to the back to check.

I just don't know what to do about this extra stock; it weighs on my mind every time I walk past the cupboard. A lot of it is seasonal so I can't sell it right now, and it feels like every Christmas I bring more out and it just looks tattier and less appealing than before.

We do have a clearance sale after Christmas each year with 20% off the seasonal stock but it never seems to shift much.

Emmanuel the e-commerce seller

One of my big strategies for last year was becoming a "one-stop shop" for design-loving individuals, and I went out and found lots of fantastic new brands to stock to help me achieve that goal.

With the fulfilment centre move, I was suddenly able to have as many products as I liked – it was like having unlimited space. I got a bit carried away.

My stock is way higher than last year, but then my sales are up too. It's hard to know how to hit the right balance between choice and stock. If I think about my stock as the money it represents instead of physical products, that's quite eye opening. I visited my fulfilment centre yesterday and just walking past the racking of my products was sobering.

I also have lumpy stock to go with my lumpy cash flow. When I order from my manufacturer, they deliver 3,000 items at once across the containers and tumblers so my stock shoots up really high.

I have been feeling the pinch lately of how much money is invested in stock but I don't know where to start with addressing the problem.

Irene the illustrator

I'm lucky in my business because I just don't have to make that much stock of most of my products. I do try to keep it controlled and print a lot of stock to order, so it helps keep down the quantities of the unproductive lines.

There are a couple of exceptions to this though. I have to print my wrapping paper in runs of 1,000 at a time, so I quite often end up with so much wrapping paper sitting in great piles in the studio!

I also had a design last year that was an update to a previous best seller. I was sure it was going to be a top seller, so I went ahead and had full print runs done of cards, prints, wrapping paper and notebooks. For some reason, the final version wasn't quite right and the customers never really took to it. Big lesson learnt there on testing before you commit to hundreds of items of something!

So, I was about to congratulate myself on not having too much unproductive stock sitting around, but then I reminded myself of those boxes in the corner and what they represent.

Controlling the tail

Managing your stock effectively is one of the most important, and most poorly understood, parts of running a product business. Overstock, or carrying too much stock as compared to your sales, is one of the major culprits when it comes to businesses running out of money or finding themselves in a situation where they can't pay their bills. It's one of the major reasons why founders find that sales are growing but they can't seem to see where the money is going.

What makes this particular issue so tricky is that it is just as likely to happen to a business that is doing well as one that is not. In fact, it is often fast-growth businesses where I find that if stock is not closely monitored, it quickly spirals out of control.

A lot of the issues revolve around the fact that there are two different types of stock – productive and unproductive. And that too much in your tail makes your business so much more unwieldy.

What people often underestimate about excess stock, or being surrounded by lots of products that aren't selling, is that excess stock sucks up more than just cash. It sucks up space and resources, such as shelving or people needed to deal with it. It takes up mental space and distracts you from the main purpose of your business, which is delighting your customers with products that they love.

There are two elements to controlling your stock. The first is identifying and managing the tail, which is what we will cover in this chapter. The second is creating a plan to avoid overspending on your stock in the future, which we'll tackle in Chapter 6.

Stock-keeping

The first part of managing your tail is to make sure that you have records of your stock. This may sound like an obvious statement, but so many product businesses do not have accurate records that are set up to keep track of what the business has in its inventory. And who can blame them? Stock-keeping has to be one of the most tedious and painstaking tasks that a business owner can do.

However, without proper records it is almost impossible to keep track of how much stock you have and as a result you won't be able to manage it effectively. If you don't know how much stock you have, you won't be able to look at what is selling and compare that to what isn't. You won't be able to see what is working.

Creating records

Part of your free Tiger Tamer's Toolkit is the stock record sheet. Go to www.resilientretailclub.com/tigertoolkit to get your copy. Get into the habit of looking at your stock at least once a month.

There are a couple of options when it comes to keeping stock records.

1. A completely manual record. Every time you bring in a product, you add it to the sheet. Once a month, you run your sales report and take the sales off from your stock. Once or twice a year, or more often if you are feeling determined to keep it accurate, you count your stock to check that your records match.

    The master list that we explored in the previous chapter can also help you create your stock records. When you keep a master list, you've got a record of everything you expect to have in terms of stock in the business, so you can make sure you don't miss anything.

    This manual approach works best if you mainly sell through one or two channels, such as your own website, or your own website and a shop.

2. You use a stock management system to help keep track of your stock.

    If you are dealing with stock across multiple platforms, it may well be worth considering investing in a stock management system. Otherwise, keeping track of everything on a spreadsheet may become extremely difficult.

    Similarly, if you are someone who has to keep track of multiple components because you are also making your products, there are stock management systems that can deal with that level of complexity and help you keep track.

    You need some method of keeping track of your stock, otherwise you will not be able to understand and analyse it.

How do you run an 80/20 analysis?

Once you have stock records, you can now run the analysis that allows you to identify where the productive stock compared to unproductive stock is to be found.

The first thing that you need to do is pick a time period for the analysis. Personally, I like to look at the last 12 weeks to give a decent snapshot. However, if that time period incorporates the Christmas period, you may find it easier to look at the run-up to Christmas as one 80/20 analysis and choose a separate time period for the rest of the calculation.

Run the data from your sales system to find out what your sales were by item. If you run a business where each item is individual – for example, a vintage or second-hand business – you may find it easier to group them into categories first.

If you sell vintage jewellery, for example, is it your earrings that produce 80% of your sales? Or necklaces? What is the category that generates most of the cash? We'll talk more about product categories later in the chapter.

If you have a clothing business, you want to make sure that you run it from the style level, in other words "ladies sweatshirt with heart print in pink" rather than looking at the different sizes individually. You can look at the 80/20 rule by size as well, but often that gets too granular for you to make sense of the data if you do it that way.

Once you have run the sales data for the time period you want to examine, use a Vlookup (refer to Chapter 4 for more information on that formula) to pull your sales information into your list of current stock.

If you get an error message as you pull the sales information in, this will suggest that you had zero sales of that item in that time period. If you don't sell an item, it won't show up on your sales reports. This is why I recommend running an 80/20 analysis based on your stock list, so that you can see where there are items that you have in stock, but which have zero sales. These will definitely be making up your tail!

Rank all of the products from highest to lowest sales. Once you have ranked them, you can work out where the 80% mark cumulatively would be.

Let's say you had sales of £4,000 for that time period. Eighty per cent of those sales is £3,200, or £4,000 multiplied by 80%. You can then highlight the cells from the top of the list until you reach that £3,200 mark. Those are your top products. Everything else below that line is your tail. If you also have your stock figures on the same sheet, then you will be able to very quickly see how much stock you have trapped in that tail and a good idea of the size of your tiger.

> Remember: the bigger the tail, the bigger the tiger.

What do you do with this analysis?

Now you have a vital and important piece of information about your business, which of your products are driving your sales?

The first thing to do, before you take a look at how much of your stock is trapped in the tail, is to make sure that you are learning the lessons from the product performance.

Best sellers – what are they telling you?

In a big retail business, the main order of the day for a Monday is a trading meeting, including the presentation of the best and worst sellers. For the many years that I worked in clothing brands, Monday morning was a flurry of activity with the junior members of the buying team hurriedly gathering up the samples – steaming and labelling them ready for the buyer to present their best and worst sellers.

It was vitally important that, as a team, we sat and reviewed what was working and what was not working. Not just as numbers on a page, but with real live products in front of us. Why was it considered so important to look at the actual product? The answer is that one of the most important tasks on an ongoing basis for a product business is to learn the lessons that your best sellers, or stars, are telling you.

Your stars are very exciting because they show you what it is that your customer wants to buy from you. It's why I strongly encourage you to take a look at them at least once a month.

Once you have identified your best sellers, ask yourself the following questions:

1. What does the customer love about this item? Is there a specific attribute, such as the fabric or the colour, or perhaps they like that price point? Do all of your best sellers, for example, sit in that £25–£30 price range which is very popular for gifting?

2. Was it the product itself that is selling well or was this the centre of your marketing this month? Are there any hints about what worked well in terms of marketing to make this the best seller? For example, was it featured in your emails? Or on your home page? Did you create a video that featured this product?

3. Are you making the most of this best seller? If you have one T-shirt design that is a best seller, do you have that T-shirt in all of the colours you could stock it in? If you have a particular colour T-shirt that seems to be doing well, are all of your designs available in that colour? What can you do to add to your product range to bring

in more similar items? If it's the price that seems to be doing well, for example, do you offer more in that price range? If a particular supplier's products are always in your best sellers, do they have any more products that you could bring in?

4. If a particular category is doing well, can you add more products from that category to your collection?

5. Did your best sellers vary between channels? Is there a difference between what the customers want to buy from you when they are buying online or in person? Does this suggest that perhaps some of your in-person best sellers are not photographed well online or do you think that there's another reason people aren't buying them?

You won't be able to answer some of these questions, but some of them will spark other thoughts. The important thing is that you are paying attention to your sales data and using it to make solid decisions. It also helps you keep an eye on the key drivers of your sales. What if you have a best seller that generates a large amount of sales and you are about to run out of it?

Keeping an eye on these figures can help you keep on top of this.

What are your worst and zero sellers telling you?

In many ways, the worst sellers are giving you just as much important information and insight as the best sellers. They are allowing you to focus on what you thought would do well but didn't.

Most small business owners, because they are investing their own money, are unlikely to buy things that they don't think will sell. But bad sales do happen! So, what went wrong between you thinking something would be a great seller and it failing to sell? Definitely take note of your gut reaction to new products and whether it was right. It's important to hone that instinct as you run your business.

Just as with the best sellers, looking at your worst sellers is important because it tells you what your customer doesn't like.

You can ask yourself similar questions to those about your best sellers, but in the inverse.

1. Are there any attributes that these worst sellers share? Colour/shape/price/product type – these are all patterns that are worth looking for.

2. Do you have other items that might share these attributes or are you planning on buying some? One of the most important things that the worst sellers can do is give us some foresight when it comes to buying other products to avoid repeating the same mistakes.

3. Do you have any more commitment on these items? For example, do you have another order coming in anytime soon? Are there things that you need to cancel if you can?

Sometimes an item has sold zero because it's not on the website yet, or is hidden away in some part of the shop or where the customer can't see it. Examining the items that have sold zero is also a useful way to catch things that are not visible to your customer for whatever reason.

Identifying the size of the tail

Now that you have taken the time to analyse the best and worst sellers, the next step with the 80/20 analysis is to identify how much stock you have in the top compared to how much you have in the tail.

How many weeks' worth of stock do you have?

One of the simplest ways to analyse your stock compared to your sales is by using a calculation known as the number of weeks' cover.

Cover is a theoretical number that shows you how many weeks' worth of stock you would have if you continued to sell at the same rate that you are currently selling at. For example, if you have 50 lampshades and you sell on average five a week, then you have 10 weeks' worth of stock left.

The calculation is:

Cover = stock/average weekly sales

In the example above,

Cover = stock/average weekly sales = 50/5 = 10 weeks' cover

This is a theoretical calculation because, in reality, it would be highly unlikely to continue to sell five lampshades a week until you hit zero. What usually happens is that as your stock sells out and the product choice is lower, then your sales also drop.

However, cover is still useful for our purposes because it gives an idea of how much stock we have compared to our sales.

You can use cover based on units, as in the example above, or you can also calculate cover based on your stock's cost value (what you paid for it) or your stock's retail value (what your customer would pay for it based on its retail price).

The most important thing is that you use the same metric for the sales and the stock. If you ran your 80/20 sales analysis based on your retail sales value, you'll need to calculate the cover based on the same.

What is the right amount of stock to have based on the number of weeks' cover? This is often the question that I get asked when I am working with clients. The answer, as with so many things, is that it depends.

We will explore ideal cover in more detail in Chapter 6 when we look at creating a stock plan, so for now we will focus on using the cover calculation to examine where we have more stock in the business than we should do.

The beauty of the cover calculation is that you can use it to evaluate everything – from looking at your products by line, all the way up to getting a snapshot of your whole business.

You can even calculate your cover by size, colour, product category or any other kind of grouping that you wish. You can also analyse one area against another. What is turning slowly and what is turning quickly?

How many weeks are in your tail?

Many businesses, once they've run the 80/20 analysis, will be able to see something that looks like this:

Average weeks' cover for the whole business is 12 weeks and total stock is £10,000.

Stars (top 80% of sales) 4 weeks' cover – total stock is £2,000.

Tail (bottom 20% of sales) 24 weeks' cover – total stock is £8,000.

Perhaps it won't be quite as drastic as that, but usually what you see is that the tail is turning much slower than the top.

Once you've identified how slow your tail is, it's a great place to start looking at how you can speed up your overall cover by clearing out the slow performers.

Depending on the size of the tail, you may not need to do anything to clear your tail other than make a note of what lines are in it, and make sure you don't buy any more of those products.

Other times, if your tail is bigger, then you are going to have to proactively take action in order to clear through some of that old stock. You may never have a situation where your tail turns as fast as your top, but you want to get that tail as small as possible. The aim of the game is for you to experiment with how little stock you can carry without impacting your sales.

Other types of stock analysis

It can be hard to make a decision based purely on a long list of products, especially if you are a business that stocks hundreds or even thousands of different lines.

In this case, it is often easier to home in on specific categories of products to see if you can see where the real problem lies.

To do this, it all comes back to your master list. If you have set it up correctly, with a category for each product, then you can easily analyse how each category is performing.

You can then look at an analysis to determine where your areas of stock are that are not moving. In order to do this, you need to create a logical product hierarchy for your business.

Product hierarchy

A product hierarchy allows you to break down your business into meaningful parts, so that you can understand not just how one particular product is selling, but how a particular category or subcategory is performing. This is an important part of you understanding how your business is working and being able to make trading decisions as you go forward.

When most people start their businesses, creating a product hierarchy is not usually on their to-do list. Many times I have worked with founders maybe three, four or five years into their business journey who want me to do more in-depth analysis of their business and it's at that point where we work together to create a product hierarchy.

If you don't have one set up right now, you are not alone. However, if you get it set up correctly, it will make it so much easier to analyse the business as you grow.

A product hierarchy starts with thinking about how your business might break down into logical chunks. Don't overthink it or make it too complicated. Less is more.

In Irene's business, she might break down her business in the following way:

Category
Cards
Prints
Textiles
Ceramics
Enamelware

Once you have those key categories identified, you can then decide on your subcategories if you feel like you have a big-enough range that you need them.

For Irene, this might look something like this:

Category	Subcategory
Cards	Mother's Day
	Father's Day
	Valentine's Day
	Christmas
	Other occasions
	Blank
	Birthday
Prints	A4 prints
	A3 prints
	Frames
Textiles	Tea towels
	Cushion covers
	Tablecloths
	Aprons
Ceramics	Mugs
	Teapots
	Egg cups
Enamelware	Trays
	Mugs
	Tins

The categories and subcategories that make sense are going to be different for every kind of business. As a good rule of thumb, if you start finding that each subcategory only has one or two products in it, then you've probably got too many. Maybe start with fewer subcategories – for example, Irene might decide to just combine Textiles, Ceramics and Enamelware into a "Homewares" category and make Textiles, Ceramics and Enamelware the subcategories.

It's better, in general, to keep things simpler, because this analysis is about you understanding the themes in your business. The benefit comes when Irene runs her sales analysis and can clearly see that her prints make up 80% of her sales and 85% of her profits. This helps her understand where she needs to focus in terms of her effort, energy and marketing. Prior to this, she might have been able to see that most of her best sellers were prints, but just from looking at a list of sales she wouldn't have been able to see so clearly what was driving her business. This is about spotting big patterns in your business and using those patterns to make decisions that will grow your sales and profits.

The best way to set up a product hierarchy is to start with a blank piece of paper and start mapping out the most useful way for you to think about your business. Once you have done this, and worked out what categories and subcategories are the most logical for you and your business, you can then start assigning each individual product a category and subcategory.

In the last chapter we talked about the "master list" or range plan – this is the perfect place to keep a record of where each product belongs in the product hierarchy. You can add in a column for category and one for subcategory, and then complete this information for every product you sell. Once completed, you'll be able to analyse where your unproductive stock lies.

You may also have the ability, depending on the system that you are using, to specify a product type within your website backend. This can make the analysis much simpler and you may even be able to run a sales and stock report directly from your website without having to go via a spreadsheet, so it's worth investigating.

Clearing slow stock

Once you have completed an 80/20 analysis and/or a product category analysis, you may well find that there are some very unproductive areas of your stock. Looking at how much you have, identifying those unproductive areas and clearing them efficiently is a process known as "clear as you go", and it's an effective method to help you avoid building up a mountain of unsold stock, like Salma's "cupboard of shame" that she describes at the beginning of the chapter.

The principle behind clearing as you go rests on a few facts:

- It's hard to let go of stock that you have paid good money for, but the faster your stock turns, the more profitable your business will be. So, it's important to move through that which is not turning.
- You need to give stock at least 8–12 weeks of sales to assess if it will sell and before you take any direct action.

Clear as you go means reviewing your stock once a month and being very clear about what is selling and what is not.

You do not have to take action every month, but you do want to be paying attention. The more that you run through your stock holding this way, the more you will begin to identify the items that are not working and make a plan to clear them.

This is not to say that you need to run a sale every month. I would suggest an absolute maximum of four clearance sales a year, with the biggest being just after Christmas/January and again in the summer, and two smaller ones at midway points between those.

Many small businesses will only run one or a maximum of two clearance events. If you manage your stock carefully throughout the year and avoid restocking poor sellers, you may even be able to get away with one small clearance event a year, or a "samples and seconds" sale to help clear out any unproductive stock.

Running a successful sale

The purpose of this clearance is not to recoup as much money as possible. It's the business equivalent of when you clean out your garage or shed. You know you paid more for a buggy than you will get for it when you sell it to a local parents' group, but you are happy to have the space back and some cash in your pocket.

That's the feeling we are going for, so don't be afraid to hit unproductive stock hard, especially if it's been hanging around for a long time.

If your in-margin is decent and your use of discounts is minimal, then the hit that your out-margin will take from deep discounting a couple of times a year will be OK.

Things to consider clearing in a stock clearance sale:

- Anything shop-soiled or damaged – but make sure that the customer is fully aware of the condition that the item is in and there aren't any nasty surprises when it arrives. You can also run these types of sales as one-offs or unique events; sample sales are often very popular.

- Ends of lines or random sizes – when you just have one or two left of something and it doesn't sit with the rest of your range.
- Pockets of stock – this is where your cover calculation comes in handy. If something is slowing down your cover or perhaps a whole subcategory is turning very slowly, this is your indication that it's time to hit it with a discount.

Running a successful sale requires planning it well in advance. Make sure you put as much care and attention into the planning and marketing of your sale as you would into the planning and marketing of a new product launch.

Make sure you are shouting about your sale as loudly as you can while it is going on, so that you can really maximize your clearance sales during that time period. Think of how high street retailers block out their entire windows with huge "Sale" posters to attract customers' attention.

What is the equivalent in your business?

What if it doesn't shift?

One of the issues that many business owners face is having stock left over after the end-of-season sale. If that happens to you, here are a few ideas:

- Is the discount that you used deep enough? When I worked in big retailers, we used to have a saying: "everything has its price". In other words, everything would sell eventually, even if you had to keep discounting it a little further each week.
- Can you keep an "outlet" section on your website to sell through a little at a time even after the sale is no longer your main focus?
- Can you make the last few days a final flash sale? Perhaps offering extra money off for loyal customers?

- Could you have another clearance channel that is separate from your main channel? If you don't want to risk your customers getting accustomed to purchasing from you at sale prices, you can set up something like an eBay account or Depop to clear through some stock at bargain prices. Keeping it separate from your main account will avoid your clearance activities being visible to your loyal customers.
- Can you donate it to charity? You can ask your accountant if there are any tax advantages to be had from donating stock.
- If something is so badly damaged that it's not saleable or in a condition that it can be donated, you may have to consider trying to dispose of it or recycle it, purely to free up space and energy. However, for most businesses this would really be the last resort.

Clearing stock and over-consumption

What if you want to minimize waste and/or don't believe in encouraging people to buy more than they should? This is an intriguing perspective and one that I've discussed with several businesses over the years.

There is a perception sometimes that this model of "clear as you go" is the antithesis of businesses that encourage lower consumption, zero waste and lower-impact forms of spending.

I totally understand this perspective, and I can also understand where people are coming from in terms of finding the idea of discounting and clearance sales uncomfortable and not aligned with their particular style of doing business.

In my experience, this belief that discounting is harmful comes from the tactics used by some big, volume retailers to either make an item appear to be a better deal than it is, or practise false scarcity or other manipulative techniques to encourage over-consumption.

Most small businesses are not set up at all in this way to compete with these types of tactics, so for them, smart discounting is about freeing up pockets of cash that have become trapped. It is like a safety valve that releases built-up pressure – but in this case it is releasing pent-up stock and cash.

It is the antithesis of discounting as a manipulative tactic that some larger retailers use – it is instead something that small businesses can use if and when it is needed.

What I will say, in this instance, is that if you feel like you want to run your business with a zero-discounting policy, I definitely support that. After all, it helps your out-margin enormously to be able to reduce the amount of discounting that you do.

However, if you want to avoid ever having to discount, you will need to be very conservative about the amount of stock that you are buying, and it becomes even more important for you to analyse your sales to see what is and is not working. The more you are tuned in to what the customer wants to buy from you, the more likely you are to be able to sell your stock at full price. You will also want to recognize quickly when your customer is not reacting to a product so that you can make sure you stop restocking it and learn your lessons from it as quickly as you can.

Our case studies

Salma the shop owner

The first thing that I had to do was tackle the cupboard of shame. One Monday (the day we are closed) I came down to the shop and pulled everything out.

As I feared, some items had got wet so I salvaged what I could. I then split the stock into two piles. Firstly, I had the items that I was going to donate to charity. I found a local organization that accepted donations from businesses and I boxed those up and called them to arrange a collection.

Everything else I decided to keep.

I realized, looking at this stock, that it was the Christmas items that were causing problems. This year I have put together a buying plan based on last year's sales, but kept it tight on the items that have very seasonal messages on them. I've also planned a stock clearance post-Christmas sale to help get rid of any remaining items so that my cupboard can remain usable all year round!

As for the rest of the stock, I've had a look at my 80/20 and a category analysis and I learnt a lot from identifying my best sellers. It's pretty much all cards when you look at the unit sales, and if you look at the cash it's all of our gifting items in the £25–£30 price range.

Because of this analysis, I've given over both of the front tables to gifting, and increased the space that we're giving to cards as well. I noticed that our clothing offering (just a few T-shirts) is definitely not producing much in the way of sales, so I've decided to stop reordering those and have reduced the space I'm giving to those in store.

Emmanuel the e-commerce seller

This has been a big piece of work but has given me some good insights into the issues in my business.

Firstly, I ran the 80/20 and it was a bit shocking because 85% of my sales were coming from about 20 products.

I had so many items that were in the "tail". The initial reaction was that perhaps I should drastically reduce the amount of products that I offered, but I felt nervous because I've literally just added the extra products in the last year.

I decided to survey my customers. I asked them what it was that they liked about shopping with me. It took me a few goes to get responses, but no-one mentioned the breadth of the offer. It was all about the aesthetic and being able to find key pieces that would make their home look stylish.

I decided to pull back on my range – not necessarily discounting them, but I marked them as "do not reorder" on my master list to help me see easily what I was selling through and not replacing. My plan at the moment is to keep selling through these lines and in about six months have a stock clearance sale to mop up anything that hasn't shifted.

I also looked at my category analysis and identified that my food storage items drive over two-thirds of my sales so when I do have some spare cash, I'm going to look at growing this area.

Irene the illustrator

When I ran my 80/20 analysis, surprise, surprise it was all of the one design that failed that was sitting there in my tail. I was shocked at the amount of cash that it represents.

I decided that these lines would be cleared in a summer sale, but since that is still a few months away, I am going to run some promotions around this product range in particular.

I'm offering a discounted bundle if you buy the whole collection, and I've also contacted my wholesale partners and asked them if they would like to purchase this collection at 20% off the wholesale price.

I appreciate that this is not making much, if anything, in terms of profits, but I am just focused on getting the products cleared through at this point.

Conclusion

As we discussed in Chapter 4 on out-margin, you are trying to maximize the amount that you sell at full price. So, while an effective stock clearance sale is a way to correct issues that have crept up over time, best practice requires you to take smaller actions more frequently.

Once a month, or at the very least once a quarter, run the 80/20 analysis. Identify the lines that are sitting in your tail. Make sure that you are gleaning what you can from this data to make sure you understand why you are sitting on this excess stock. Decide what it is that you want to do to help you clear it.

a. Nothing – you are going to let it sell through.

b. Some action now – running a discount or targeted offer on certain products.

c. Run a stock clearance sale.

The other key area here is looking at the categories and subcategories that make up your business to help you understand what is, and isn't, working for your business.

Ultimately, identifying the tail can help you enormously when it comes to keeping your stock at a reasonable level for your business. Identifying what that reasonable level looks like, and how to monitor it as you move forward, is the subject of the next chapter.

Key points

- Every product business carries a mixture of productive and unproductive stock.
- The unproductive stock is called the tail, and the bigger the tail, the bigger the tiger.
- The more stock you have that is turning slowly, the more likely you are to have cash flow and profitability problems.
- Running an 80/20 analysis is a quick way to get a handle on where you have pockets of unproductive stock that you can then clear.
- You can also look at other types of analysis such as analysing the category of stock to help you see where your unprofitable stock is sitting.
- Go to www.resilientretailclub.com/tigertoolkit to get a template for your stock records.
- The 'Additional resources' section details further support you can get with the concepts in this chapter.

Over to you

1. Update the stock in your master list or, at the very least, run your stock report so you know how much stock you have in the business.

2. Pull in your sales to create your 80/20 analysis.

3. Use the cover calculation to work out how much stock you have in your tail.

4. What are you going to do about it?
   a. Nothing – just focus on not rebuying that stock.
   b. Actively clear at a clearance sale at some point in the future, e.g. post Christmas or in the summer.
   c. Run some type of spotlight or offer on the slow stock to move it through.

CHAPTER 6

THE TAIL – CREATING A PLAN

How much stock should I have?

This is one of the most commonly asked questions that I get from product businesses because, after all, who starts a product business fully equipped with a good understanding of the ideal amount of stock to hold?

It's an important question to ask when you are trying to control your tail because it has a direct impact on how much money is tied up in your business. If you have a small amount of stock and some of it is unproductive, you will have a small tail. If you have a lot of stock, and a lot of it is unproductive, you will have a big tail, and a big problem! Remember – the bigger the tail, the bigger the tiger.

As with so many of these types of questions, the answer to "how much stock should I have?" is "it depends". Getting the right amount of stock for the size of your business is a combination of how much you think you are going to sell, how quickly you can get more and perhaps a little bit to do with the size of your physical space (if you have one).

Not least, it depends on where you are starting from as a business. If you currently have enough stock to last your business for two years (not unheard of!) then aiming for four weeks is going to be a tough slog.

The key, however, is to create a plan, which is the focus of this chapter. Once you have a plan, even a simple one, you can start to put the pieces together in terms of how much you should be buying at any one time. It can give you the confidence to make decisions about purchasing without that sick feeling of having way too much invested in stock.

Visit www.resilientretailclub.com/tigertoolkit for a checklist and video to help you get started on creating a stock plan.

Our case studies

Salma the shop owner

I think this is one of the hardest elements for me – working out how much stock I should have and therefore how much I'm going to buy. Sometimes I buy an item as a trial, and then before I know it, it's sold out and I have to place a reorder, but there's a £300 minimum order for that brand, so I end up over-ordering and the money feels like it's going straight out again.

I try to have a budget but it is hard to know whether or not I've done it right. I don't feel like I've got any visibility. I do keep track of my invoices – as I pay them, I keep a record – but that doesn't help me feel any better about the situation.

Emmanuel the e-commerce seller

My stock outlay is one of the biggest issues with my cash flow. I tend to buy on gut rather than with any kind of strategy in place. I'm always seeing lovely new things that I think would be perfect for the shop and I tend to spend first and ask questions later. Even though my overheads are not that high, I spend all and any spare cash on stock.

I get nervous about taking money out of the business to pay myself because I worry about what will happen if I want to buy some more stock and there isn't the cash to cover it.

Irene the illustrator

The massive growth that we've undergone has made it so hard to keep track of our stock and I know that we have so much more than last year. During our fastest growth periods we kept selling out within a few minutes of launch so we made the decision to buy much larger quantities, which also helped us get better prices from the suppliers as well.

There's definitely no plan – as long as the sales are coming in, we're just buying.

I feel like we're flying blind. We are running to catch up with demand but at the same time, the shelves in our unit are getting full and we only put the racking in last year! We've been talking about adding a mezzanine level to the warehouse but I just wonder if we're being busy fools.

Doing the 80/20 analysis is helpful to identify where all this extra stock is sitting and get us thinking about clearing out slow sellers. I still don't feel sure about how to plan what we can buy.

What is a stock plan?

Identifying and managing the tail, which we covered in the previous chapter, is an important part of avoiding your stock building up in the wrong places over time.

One of the other challenges that many businesses face is not knowing how much stock they should even have to begin with. In an ideal world, businesses should know how much stock they need to have overall and then work to reduce the unproductive stock, so that they have less stock overall, and also the stock that they do have is working harder.

The advantage of having a stock budget is that there is a clear amount that you know you need to have in your business to hit your sales goal, and it can also help you avoid overspending. Think of it like a household budget. Many people have a plan on how much they can spend on different things, like food shopping or days out, to help them stay within pre-decided limits. A stock budget for your business is exactly the same.

Stock budgets are a huge part of the buying process in large companies. The purse strings, or OTB (open to buy) amounts, were controlled by the merchandisers and helped the buyers and designers understand what the limits were in terms of how much they could spend.

This wasn't some hypothetical limit that we stuck to if we tried; it was a very real number that we had to stick to. If we were over the limit, we had to look at every way possible to reduce the stock. We might have to delay orders or put on stock-clearing promotions to work through unproductive stock. We also had to explain to the buying teams that the new products they wanted to bring in right away would have to wait, which never went down well!

Each month, I would have to report to the executive team how much stock we had compared to how much we were supposed to have. If a team regularly exceeded the planned amount of stock without a very good reason, the merchandiser didn't keep their job for long. That's how seriously big retailers take their stock limits.

For small retailers, often there is no stock budget, so when things don't sell or old stock starts to build up, there are no red flags being waved or alarms being sounded. And yet, having too much stock is one of the fundamental reasons that product businesses have problems with their cash flow.

Remember to think about your products as piles of cash instead of physical products – it's then very easy to understand why too much stock chokes your bottom line.

If you can create yourself a stock plan, you too can have this monthly focus on whether or not you have the right amount (or too much) stock in your business. While you won't be at risk of being fired if you do, it will give you a clear number to work towards and help you understand how much you can afford to be holding in stock.

Shiny new stock syndrome

Shiny new stock syndrome, as I jokingly call it, is the condition where a business owner becomes convinced that the only way to grow their sales is to bring in more stock. Occasionally, when someone has an extremely small range, it can be helpful to expand and bring in a wider range of products. However, it is also very easy to fall into the trap that says that if you keep on buying new products, the big turning point for your business is round the corner.

Often, all this does is pile up stock and create more of a build-up. If you feel that you absolutely do need new products to come in to drive sales, do you know what you are planning on doing with the rest?

Having a stock plan helps focus your mind and if you do indulge in shiny new stock, at least you can make sure that you do it within predefined parameters and a solid budget!

How do you create a stock plan?

There are many ways to create a stock plan, and it can be as simple or as complex as you like. In big retailers, the stock plans are run in dedicated software, although a surprisingly large number, controlling millions of pounds, are run in Excel, often printed on multiple A3 pieces of paper in the tiniest print. They are set up on a week-by-week basis and are known as a WSSI – weekly sales and stock intake.

However, for small business owners, this level of complexity is not only unattainable, it's not needed. It is best to start with something extremely simple – a monthly stock budget.

Let's imagine that this is a stock plan created by Emmanuel the e-commerce seller. Assume that this is in £, and that the figures we are looking at represent the retail sales value of the stock.

Month	Opening stock	Sales plan	Dis-counts	Ideal closing stock	Con-firmed intake	Amount available to spend	Actual closing stock
January	10,000	3,000	390	12,000	3,000	2,390	12,000
February	12,000	3,500	455	12,000	1,500	2,455	12,000
March	12,000	4,000	520	12,000		4,520	12,000
April	12,000	3,500	455	12,000		3,955	12,000
May	12,000	3,500	455	12,000		3,955	12,000
June	12,000	3,500	455	12,000		3,955	12,000
July	12,000	3,000	390	12,000		3,390	12,000
August	12,000	2,500	325	12,000		2,825	12,000
September	12,000	4,500	585	12,000		5,085	12,000
October	12,000	6,000	780	19,000		13,780	19,000
November	19,000	9,000	1,170	15,000		6,170	15,000
December	15,000	7,000	910	12,000		4,910	12,000

If you look at this and get that "hot flush of fear" that we talked about at the start of the book, do not worry. Although there are many numbers, each one is very logical and we are going to walk them through in detail.

If you do need more help with the stock plan, check the 'Additional resources' section at the end of this book.

To help create your own stock plan, let's go through the columns one by one.

Month

This stock plan is set up by month. You can choose whichever time frame you like, whether that's the calendar year (January to December), the tax year (April to March) or your business financial year if it's different from both of these. However, I do suggest that you look at this plan over 12 months to help you understand how your stock needs might change over time.

Once you have chosen the time frame you want to use going forward, start where you are now. If you are reading this book in May, for example, and you are going to use January to December as your time frame, start populating from May onwards. If you can get the historic data about stock value and sales from previous months, that would be ideal, but if that's too hard to get, then just go ahead and work forwards.

Opening stock

The opening stock for a month is the same as the closing stock for the previous month. So January closing stock becomes February opening stock. The only reason that I put it in as a separate column is because I find it easier for many people to grasp what is happening in each month when they start with the opening stock position.

Most months, the opening stock is just a calculation, where you make it equal to your closing stock from the previous month; however, the first month that you start your stock plan, you will need to type in the opening stock number for that month from your stock records.

Sales plan

Your first in-depth task when it comes to the stock plan is creating a sales plan, or forecast by month. Why does a stock plan start with a sales plan? Because the question of how much stock you should have is based on how much you think you should sell.

Hopefully you already have a sales plan by month because there are many advantages to having set a sales goal for the business even apart from needing one to create a stock plan. However, if you don't have a sales plan, you need to create one.

People often tell me that they do not know where to begin with a sales plan, but it's often simpler than you think. One of the most misunderstood elements of forecasting is that the purpose of the plan is not to be right but to create a framework that you can work around.

It is very rare, if not impossible, for you to sell the exact amount that you plan for a month, so don't get hung up on picking the exact number. Start with a realistic plan and adjust accordingly.

How do you start with a realistic plan? Well, there are usually two key elements – your sales history and how you are doing now, also known as the "run rate".

To get your plan, you want to combine the history and the run rate together.

Let's say, for example, last year your sales looked like this:

	Last year
January	£2,000
February	£2,333
March	£2,667

However, when you look at the last three months, your sales have been 50% up. One simple way to forecast your sales is to take last year's sales pattern and add 50%.

	Last year	Add 50% run rate	Total
January	£2,000	£1,000	£3,000
February	£2,333	£1,167	£3,500
March	£2,667	£1,333	£4,000

This would give you a good starting point. You can of course adjust things if you know that, for example, last year's February was terrible because you had major supply issues, you might want to increase February above the number that is generated.

I always think that these numbers should feel like an exciting target but not too much of a stretch that they feel unworkable or paralysing. Sometimes you need to put in the figures and allow them to generate based on the run rate and the history, and then amend them to create a series of sales targets that you feel comfortable and confident aiming for.

The most important thing, above all else, is that you don't spend so long tweaking these numbers that you never finish the stock plan. It's far better to put in numbers quickly that you think look logical, and then adjust as you go along, rather than endlessly tinkering with your sales plan.

Discounts

The discount column has to be included because any discounts you offer affect the amount of stock you have left at the end of the month.

If you have a pen worth £10, and you sell it at 50% off, you have sales of £5 and a discount amount of £5. Once you have sold it, you are left with zero stock, because that £10 is devalued by the £5 discount and then you sell it for £5. When it comes to stock calculations, you have to take into account the amount of discount in order to make the whole thing work.

If you're not sure what the discount amount should be, I suggest using a blended average based on past history. In Emmanuel's stock plan, he assumed a 13% discount amount each month due to his history.

You may also want to play around with the discount level by month – for example, it is likely to be higher in the months that you run clearance sales. However, like the sales plan, do not spend too much time trying to perfectly forecast your discount level by month. Far better to put in a logical amount and tweak over time.

Ideal closing stock

Your ideal stock is the amount of stock that you want to have in your business at the end of each month in order to have enough to cover your sales but simultaneously avoid having so much that all your cash is tied up.

Think of it as a stake in the ground – a number that you want to do whatever you can to avoid exceeding. Putting this stake in the ground and working around it starts making you think differently about your stock and is one of the most effective ways to stop you overspending on stock.

This column in many ways is the most important one in the stock plan because this is the number that determines how much you can spend each month. However, you may be wondering how on earth you decide what that number should be.

As with most things to do with stock, your ideal closing stock for each month should be related to your sales. How many weeks' worth of stock do you want to hold at any one time?

To help you figure this out, you can look at the number of weeks' cover that we briefly touched on in the previous chapter.

To calculate cover, you use the following formula:

Number of weeks' cover = total amount of stock/average weekly sales

If Emmanuel had £15,000 of stock at retail value, and his average weekly sales were £1,000 a month, then his actual number of weeks' cover would be 15.

Number of weeks' cover = £15,000 divided by £1,000 = 15

Setting the number of weeks' cover you want in your business allows you to reverse engineer the ideal stock.

Let's say Emmanuel decides that 12 weeks is ideal, then he can use a formula to determine his ideal closing stock:

Ideal closing stock = desired weeks' cover × average weekly sales

Ideal closing stock = 12 weeks' cover × £1,000 = £12,000

This all comes back to setting the ideal number of weeks' cover. How many weeks should it be?

Realistically, the number that is right for your business comes down to a few factors.

1. What is your starting point? If you are currently on 400 weeks' cover, then setting it at 25 is going to mean that you can't bring new stock in for months. You would want to bring it down over time.

2. How long does it take to get new stock in? If you can get new stock delivered from your supplier in a matter of days, do you need to hold two months' worth of stock? And if you can get more stock in six weeks, do you need to have six months?

This is all about hitting a balance between having the least amount of stock possible and leaving money on the table because you don't have something that your customer wants.

Sometimes what you need to do is play around with a few different weeks' cover numbers to work out what your ideal closing stock should be. Remember, once you have decided on the number of weeks' cover that you want, you can use that to create an ideal closing stock.

Ideal closing stock = desired weeks' cover × average weekly sales

Once you have that number as a cash amount, you will need to make a few further decisions.

Firstly, you'll notice that since your sales are different each month, that will in theory give you a different ideal closing stock for each month. This is useful to know, and it can help you get a sense of how your need for stock changes throughout the year, especially as you build towards a peak selling period like Christmas.

However, you may want to decide whether or not you want your ideal closing stock to stay the same most of the time except during peak periods. This is worth considering because it often helps businesses to have a consistent amount of stock to avoid major fluctuations in the amount of space that they need for storage, and it also simplifies the plan.

As you get more used to running a stock plan, you may decide you want to play around more with your ideal closing stock so that you need even less during quieter months.

Consider Emmanuel's plan that we saw at the beginning of the chapter:

Month	Opening stock	Sales plan	Dis-counts	Ideal closing stock	Con-firmed intake	Amount available to spend	Actual closing stock
January	10,000	3,000	390	12,000	3,000	2,390	12,000
February	12,000	3,500	455	12,000	1,500	2,455	12,000
March	12,000	4,000	520	12,000		4,520	12,000
April	12,000	3,500	455	12,000		3,955	12,000
May	12,000	3,500	455	12,000		3,955	12,000
June	12,000	3,500	455	12,000		3,955	12,000
July	12,000	3,000	390	12,000		3,390	12,000
August	12,000	2,500	325	12,000		2,825	12,000
September	12,000	4,500	585	12,000		5,085	12,000
October	12,000	6,000	780	19,000		13,780	19,000
November	19,000	9,000	1,170	15,000		6,170	15,000
December	15,000	7,000	910	12,000		4,910	12,000

Most months have an ideal closing stock of £12,000, except for October and November which are higher to accommodate the Christmas rush. By the end of December, Emmanuel is planning for the closing stock to be back down to its typical level ready to enter into a quieter sales period.

Once you have played around with the ideal closing stock, you will be most of the way towards having a clear stock budget and using that number to identify how much you can spend on stock each month.

Confirmed intake

This column is your place to record what you already have committed to ordering. Let's say that Emmanuel has seen some vases that he likes and placed an order worth £1500 that is coming in the following month. That is what he would add to his confirmed intake column. The number that goes into the column for each month is the total of all the confirmed orders that you have coming from all your suppliers.

It's important to put this into the plan because how much money you have to spend on new stock is directly impacted by how much you already have coming in. You need to have a space that captures this so that as you confirm orders and record them in that column, you can see it reducing the amount you have to spend.

In terms of how to manage this on a practical level, I suggest that you need a simple log of every invoice for every stock order you place, including the retail value of those products, and add for each invoice which month it will arrive in. You can then update the stock plan with your committed intake for that month. You may want to do this regularly, so that as you are planning other orders you have an updated idea of how much you have available to spend.

The other useful function of the confirmed intake column is that when you are planning on placing orders, you can play around with adding them into this column to see what impact they will have on your stock levels before agreeing to the purchase with a supplier.

Amount available to spend

As the name suggests, this column will guide you on how much you can spend each month on stock. It is one of the most important numbers in the plan because this is your budget you have to play with.

It is based on a calculation. The way that the calculation works is comparing what your actual closing stock would be compared to your ideal stock.

> Amount available to spend = Ideal closing stock – (this month's opening stock – the sales plan for the month – the discount amount + any confirmed intake)

If we look at the month of February in the example above, the numbers look like this:

Amount available to spend = £12,000 – (£12,000 – £3,500 – £455 + £1,500) = £12,000 – £9,545 = £2,455

The number in this column should never be less than zero. If you use the template version in the Tiger Tamer course (see the Additional Resources section for more details) then it has a formula that automatically rounds up if the number is zero; otherwise, if you are making your own version, keep an eye out for any negative numbers and make them zero.

Similarly, if you are in January and the plan shows that you have money to spend on stock in that month, but you know that you cannot physically get stock in until March because of your supplier lead time, make sure you make that amount you have to spend that month zero to indicate that you won't have stock coming in until later.

Several factors impact how much you have to spend in any given month:

- Whether or not you started the month over your ideal stock – in this example, every month ends where it is

     supposed to, but if you started with far more stock
     than ideal, you might not be able to spend anything
     for quite some time.

- What your sales and discount levels are planned to be.
- How much stock you already have committed to for that particular month.

What is most important with this column is that you can use it for your purchasing so that you no longer feel that you have no idea of how much you should be spending. Instead, you can see, down to the nearest £, what your remaining budget is for that month.

It should also help you when you have to place larger orders in advance, for example securing your Christmas stock. You'll see how much you can spend and be able to allocate funds accordingly.

One of the most important skills that you will learn as a business owner is how to make best use of the amount you have available to spend each month. You will have some clear priorities, for example, re-buying best sellers that are low on stock, so you must make sure you have enough money for these crucial purchases. As far as possible, you want to avoid over-committing the amount you have available to spend on products that are untested. Tying up most of your available cash on a large order of something with no selling history is risky at best. Far better to take an approach called "test and learn".

Test and learn involves purchasing a small quantity of an untried item, even if you have to pay a higher cost price than you would if you bought it at volume. Once you have seen how the customer reacts to that item, you can place a second, larger top-up order with far more confidence than if you had no data to base your decision on at all.

Actual closing stock

The final column is a calculation of what the actual stock will be at the end of the month as opposed to the ideal stock.

> Actual closing stock = opening stock – sales – discounts + confirmed intake + amount available to spend

In an ideal world, and as in the first version of Emmanuel's stock plan above, your closing stock and ideal stock would be the sale. However, that is unlikely to be the case for many people.

Let's look at what would happen if Emmanuel already had far too much stock in his business:

Month	Opening stock	Sales plan	Dis-counts	Ideal closing stock	Con-firmed intake	Amount available to spend	Actual closing stock
January	25,000	3,000	390	12,000	3,000	0	24,610
February	24,610	3,500	455	12,000	1,500	0	22,155
March	22,155	4,000	520	12,000		0	17,635
April	17,635	3,500	455	12,000		0	13,680
May	13,680	3,500	455	12,000		2,275	12,000
June	12,000	3,500	455	12,000		3,955	12,000
July	12,000	3,000	390	12,000		3,390	12,000
August	12,000	2,500	325	12,000		2,825	12,000
September	12,000	4,500	585	12,000		5,085	12,000
October	12,000	6,000	780	19,000		13,780	19,000
November	19,000	9,000	1,170	15,000		6,170	15,000
December	15,000	7,000	910	12,000		4,910	12,000

Just changing the amount of his opening stock in January from £10,000 in the first example to £25,000 in this example means that there is no money available to spend until May, when his stock levels drop down to the ideal level again.

The actual closing stock column is also useful when it comes to stock takes – you'll have an actual number to compare to when it comes to looking at how much stock is in the business!

Working with stock plans

Now you have your nice neat stock plan, that's all the hard work done, right?

While you may be feeling, and rightfully so, very pleased with yourself for creating a stock plan to help you budget your stock purchasing, the real beauty of this plan is that it is not a one-time exercise that you do at the start of the year and then file away, never to be seen again. It's a living, breathing tool that you can use throughout your year and adjust according to what happens in your business.

Remember when I said that the purpose of your plan is not to be right, but to be a framework? That is fortunate because it never will be exactly right!

Each month you will have a sales plan, and that will impact how much you have available to spend going forward.

However, you are going to need to adjust this as you go along, either when sales are better or worse than planned.

Let's look at Emmanuel's plan as he starts to trade it. Firstly, he makes himself a copy of the original plan so he always has it to refer back to. Now he starts updating it.

Here's the original plan for his first quarter:

Month	Opening stock	Sales plan	Dis-counts	Ideal closing stock	Con-firmed intake	Amount available to spend	Actual closing stock
January	25,000	3,000	390	12,000	3,000	0	24,610
February	24,610	3,500	455	12,000	1,500	0	22,155
March	22,155	4,000	520	12,000		0	17,635

After January has finished, he goes into his working copy and updates the figures with what happened:

Month	Opening stock	Sales plan	Dis-counts	Ideal closing stock	Con-firmed intake	Amount available to spend	Actual closing stock
January	25,000	5,000	1,400	12,000		0	18,600
February	18,600	3,500	455	12,000	1,500	0	16,145
March	16,145	4,000	520	12,000		375	12,000

After realizing how much stock he had compared to the ideal, he decided to heavily promote his "tail" and as result both his sales and discount level were much higher than expected.

He also had the opportunity to get out of the stock due in January as the supplier had a quality issue and informed him they were unable to fulfil his order.

All of this combined meant that his stock was much lower than anticipated by the end of January, which opened up a small amount of money available to spend in March.

In February, when he updated the plan, it wasn't quite positive. Emmanuel had been away for two weeks and hadn't done much to drive the business as he didn't have time to schedule any social media or emails while away.

In addition, he felt that several of his most loyal customers had bought a lot during the sale and as a result were not as willing to buy in February.

He had not bought the amount in March that showed as being available to spend, which was fortunate because after February's sales results, he was still showing as being overstocked in March.

Month	Opening stock	Sales plan	Dis- counts	Ideal closing stock	Con- firmed intake	Amount available to spend	Actual closing stock
January	25,000	5,000	1,400	12,000		0	18,600
February	18,600	2,313	100	12,000	1,500	0	17,687
March	17,687	4,000	520	12,000	0	0	13,167

When used correctly, a stock plan is the closest thing that you will have to a crystal ball in your business. You will be able to tell in January that you are going to run out of stock in June, or see in March that you are going to be building up too much stock by October.

There are so many things that you can see using a stock plan that its true worth comes into play as you trade through and review it once a month.

It is a powerful practice to get into where you set up a sales plan, then examine it every month and make adjustments going forward.

When sales exceed expectations

When sales are doing better than you planned, ask yourself the following questions:

- What is driving this success? Is it specific products or is the whole business doing better than expected?

- Do I need to order more of the best sellers, or the supplies to make these items?
- Can my current supply base keep up with demand or do I need to start thinking about finding an additional supplier to keep up?
- Are there any orders I have scheduled for later on in the year that I can ask to have earlier?
- How can I build on the success of the sales? Am I making the most of the best sellers?
- Where are these sales coming from? What is the most effective way I am currently marketing and promoting my business?
- Do my current sales plans for future months look high enough or should I be increasing them to get an accurate view of how much stock I might need in future months?
- Is my ideal closing stock still looking correct or do I need more stock now that sales are growing? Am I still happy with the number of weeks' cover that this figure represents?

When sales underperform

If your sales are below expectations:

- What can I do to drive these sales? Am I doing absolutely everything I can think of to get my business out there in front of the customer?
  - Do I need to look again at my marketing plans and activities?
  - Are my current marketing channels/content strategies working?
  - Have I exhausted every way of promoting my business? Any leads I haven't followed up?
- What isn't working? Are there items that are clogging up my stock number that I need to take care of?

- Am I going to take action to clear some of that stock?
- Are there any orders that I can cancel without a penalty and without putting my supplier in a difficult position if I'm going to be overstocked? (These would either be orders from a third party who will be able to reallocate stock if you don't take it, or if your manufacturer has not actually purchased the materials to start your order yet.)
- Can I delay any orders that I can't cancel?
- Do my sales plans for future months look correct or do I need to bring them down to accurately assess how much stock I need?
- Is my ideal closing stock still looking correct or do I need less stock now that sales are lower? Am I still happy with the number of weeks' cover that this figure represents?

Having a plan with a fixed amount of stock that you don't want to exceed means that your thought process shifts. It becomes focused on how to most efficiently deal with the stock that you have rather than looking at bringing more in and ignoring the stock piling up.

Our case studies

Salma the shopkeeper

This was such a good exercise for me. I already had a sales forecast as I use it with the team to motivate them and keep the focus on selling. It was relatively easy for me to put together a budget based on sales.

It's taken a bit of time to get used to the whole stock plan, but I do feel a lot more in control of what I'm doing. I'm tracking all of my invoices and adding up how much I'm spending each month.

This is making me focus on selling what I've got instead of always feeling like I've got to be bringing in the new, and I just love having an actual figure to work towards each month.

Emmanuel the e-commerce seller

I had real mixed feelings about this process. On the one hand, I instantly felt much better just knowing how much stock I have in the business and having a clear idea of what I thought I should be selling.

However, it was not easy. I have about 25 weeks' cover based on current sales, which is nearly six months of stock! I felt bad about that for a while until I realized that I just had no way of knowing or measuring how much stock I should have so that helped me feel less guilty.

Obviously at the moment it's saying that I don't need any stock for ages so I'm looking at how I can push some of the slow areas to help me sell through.

I do feel a bit like it's taken some of the fun away for me – I saw some beautiful vases I wanted to buy and I had to tell myself no for now. I might give myself a little pot of fun money so I can still bring in small amounts of lovely things.

I wanted to know where all my money was going, and that's become abundantly clear, so I have to buckle down now and do the work to wrestle control of this tiger.

Irene the illustrator

It was quite comforting doing this exercise for a couple of reasons. Firstly, I put in an actual sales plan for the first time ever and it immediately helped with everything – from the conversations that we were having with our ads agency to working out how many boxes we should be ordering.

The stock part was illuminating – it's around eight weeks' cover, which doesn't seem bad. However, it did make me question why our paper goods were on eight weeks' cover when we can get those from the printer in under two weeks. I decided to set a target of six weeks for those going forward, and leave the fabric items at 10 weeks because they take that much longer to come in from the supplier.

Between the stock budget and the stock analysis, I feel so much more on top of what we've got. I think we can definitely reduce some stock, especially in the areas that I have identified as problematic, but equally we do need a lot of stock to fuel our sales!

I feel a lot clearer about what I need to look at and understand how I can adjust our plans if we exceed our sales targets, or even if we drop below them. I also feel that clearing out some of our unproductive stock will probably mean we do not need the mezzanine floor in the warehouse just yet!

Conclusion

While mapping out your stock budgets may not feel like the most important task for your business given all of the other demands, it is a key piece of taming your tiger. Creating the budget, trading it according to how your business is performing, in combination with running and knowing your 80/20 analysis, can be transformative for your business.

All of a sudden, your stock stops being one big lump that you can't control, sucking up your money. You gain an in-depth understanding of where your money is and how to work with it to free up trapped cash. In addition, you also get excellent visibility of future problems, long before they happen! It is well worth the time and effort required to get this information.

Once you've got control of your stock, which is the biggest expense for product businesses, it's time to turn your attention to the other expenses in your business, which we will cover in the next chapter.

Key points

- As well as needing to know where the unprofitable stock is, it's very beneficial to have a stock plan, which first requires you to have a sales plan.
- Once you have that, you can use it, along with your desired cover, to create an ideal closing stock and stock budget for each month that you can adjust according to how your business is performing each month.
- There are many ways to make stock plans work for your business. Once you have got used to working with one, you may want to consider all the ways you can make it tailored to your business.

Over to you

1. Looking at the stock plan, set up one of your own. You can visit www.resilientretailclub.com/tigertoolkit for a checklist and video to help you get started, or further help with these concepts can be found in the 'Additional resources' section at the end of the book.

2. Walk through the steps outlined in this chapter to create your plan.

3. Decide on a day each month that you will update your stock plan. Can you see how you will be able to use this on an ongoing basis?

4. How has the exercise made you feel about how much stock you have in your business?

5. Once you have set this plan up, would you consider having more than one for your business? For example, depending on your business, you could have:

   a. A stock plan for your website and one for your store.

   b. A stock plan for different product types, e.g. one for Christmas stock and one for non-seasonal items or for different categories within your business.

   c. A stock plan for your wholesale business vs. your direct-to-customer business.

   d. You could create a unit stock plan if that makes more sense for you than retail value – it works exactly the same way but everything is calculated in units. This might make sense if you have both a wholesale and direct-to-consumer business that you want to look at together.

   e. You could create a stock plan based only on the cost of the products – as with the unit stock plan, it works the same way but everything is in cost value not retail.

This is covered in more detail within the Tiger Tamer course but once you start using the plan and see the value, there are so many opportunities for you to tailor it to your particular business model.

CHAPTER 7

THE STOMACH

Now we arrive at the final part of the tiger-taming journey – the stomach. How much are you feeding your tiger? A tiger business is a hungry beast. It will never tell you when it's had enough, and it is always ready to eat up more of your money. You need your own guidelines for how much your business needs.

Most of the time when I work with product businesses, the main issues are related to the teeth and the tail. After all, stock is one of the biggest expenses that a product business has, so it's not too surprising that this is where many people's problems lie.

However, the fixed costs, or how much you are feeding your tiger each month, can often be a source of huge frustration and worry for product business owners.

Whether it's never feeling like there's enough money to pay for sufficient help or being unable to judge how sensible it is to be spending the money that they are paying out, fixed overheads are hard for many product owners to grapple with.

Visit www.resilientretailclub.com/tigertoolkit to get a checklist of costs needed to create the analysis in this chapter.

Our case studies

Salma the shop owner

One of the biggest challenges of running a shop is that my overheads are fixed and fairly substantial.

As well as my rent, I have rates and utilities, plus I need a certain level of staffing to keep the shop open. Most of the time I try to have two people in the shop, otherwise it makes it so challenging for the one person who's in the store all alone and can't even run to the loo without closing the store!

That's fine, but as a result, it means that there isn't much room to manoeuvre. Of course there are seasonal fluctuations in sales, but there isn't much flexibility to reduce costs at slow times. I have to cover my overheads at the very least.

Emmanuel the e-commerce seller

I have tried to build my business in such a way that my fixed costs each month are comfortable. I do have a fulfilment centre now, but the benefit with that is that other than a monthly storage and management fee, I pay them picking fees, which means that if I'm not selling as much, I'm not paying as much.

I work from home, so there are no fees for offices or studios. I do most of the jobs in the business myself – customer service emails, social media scheduling, things like that. I don't have a huge outlay on that front. The one exception is my ads manager who I pay £1,000 a month, plus a budget of £3,000 to spend on the ads themselves.

Of course, I pay all the regular fees around website hosting, email marketing etc., but other than the ads, my overall outgoings are pretty low.

Irene the illustrator

This is definitely the most difficult part of my business for me – my overheads.

Last year we were feeling so squeezed in the house, and I was beginning to feel like I had no time or space for anything other than the business, so we made the decision to move to a commercial unit.

I have no issue with the idea of getting a unit; that definitely wasn't a mistake. In many ways it was a fabulous decision. The issue is that the one I was talked into was far too big and expensive. I rushed the process and was so caught up in the idea of having my own space that I took the first one I was offered.

To make matters worse, I have now found that my heating bills (which, unbeknownst to me, were not included in the price I was quoted) have gone up by around 50%, so it feels like I have so much I have to sell before I have even broken even. Given that my prices are low, it sometimes feels like I have to sell a whole mountain of products before I even break even.

My team costs have also gone up too, partly because now that we are working from the unit, I feel the need to have someone here all day because our courier pick-ups are not consistent. I'm worried that one day we'll miss the pick-up because we're not there.

I regret increasing my outgoings to the extent that I did. Before the unit, I always had a nice buffer each month, and now it feels like I'm living hand to mouth.

Are you feeding your tiger too much?

As businesses grow, so do the costs associated with those sales. Many business owners that I speak to find it very difficult to gauge exactly how much they can afford to spend on fixed costs based on their sales. They may even find themselves awake at night trying to figure out if they have over-extended themselves.

In my experience, many business owners find it hard to create and maintain an accurate cash-flow model unless they have a lot of assistance from their accountant, specialist software or previous experience in this type of financial modelling.

However, many can create a simpler model for themselves to help understand their break-even point – the sales number which allows them to cover all the fixed costs in a business. This type of model, which I call a break-even analysis, is reasonably simple to create, especially once you have a good understanding of the numbers in your business such as your out-margin that we discussed in Chapter 4.

What I like most about a break-even analysis is that it also allows you to model the impact of increasing your business costs before you commit to them.

A break-even analysis

First we're going to look at an example of a break-even analysis, this time from Irene's business, and then we'll walk through each element so you can start thinking about preparing one for your own business.

You can visit www.resilientretailclub.com/tigertoolkit to get your free tool kit, including a checklist of all the expenses to include in your break-even analysis.

Irene the illustrator's break-even analysis

Average monthly sales including VAT	£28,000
Excluding VAT	£23,333
Out-margin	60%
Retail gross profit	£14,000
Cost of premises incl utilities	£3,000
Staff costs	£3,500
Owner salary	£2,500
Marketing costs	£3,000
Other business costs	£900
Total costs	£12,900
Remainder	£1,100

It is a positive picture. Irene has, in an average month, enough profit being generated to pay herself and have money left over.

Let's break down each section in more detail.

Average monthly sales including VAT

This number will come from Irene's sales plan we discussed in Chapter 5 – she can take an average of what she is forecasting as her sales across the next 12 months.

Sales excluding VAT

If you are not VAT registered, you will not need a separate line for your sales excluding VAT. If you are VAT registered, you need to divide your average monthly sales by 1.2 to remove the VAT.

Out-margin

This is the number you will have calculated in Chapter 4. It represents the average profit you make in your business after all product-related expenses. The higher it is, the more money you will be left with from your sales to cover any other expenses.

If you have wholesale and retail sales, and both sales channels are significant for your business, you may find it easier at this point to put in a sales forecast for each channel, with an associated out-margin for each, and then combine it into one.

Irene's might look like this:

	Wholesale	Retail	Total
Average monthly sales including VAT	£8,537	£19,463	£28,000
Excluding VAT	£7,114	£16,220	£23,333
Out-margin	35%	71%	60%
Retail gross profit	£2,490	£11,510	£14,000

Retail gross profit

This is an estimate of the amount of profit you will be making in an average month as a result of your sales and your out-margin. It is calculated as follows:

> Retail gross profit = sales (exc. VAT) × out-margin

In this case, the calculation would be: £23,333 × 60% = £14,000

Essentially, your retail gross profit is the amount of money that you have available to cover all of your fixed costs.

Fixed costs

This section is where you add up all of the fixed costs associated with running your business. One of the easiest ways to make sure you capture everything is to run through your business bank account and look at which payments come out every month.

If you have a cost that you only have to pay once a year, you can divide it by 12 to give you a monthly figure you can use.

Here are some of the fixed costs to consider:

Costs of premises and utilities

This is where you would include all of the costs that you have associated with your business premises, including:

Rent
Service charge
Rates
Gas
Water
Electricity
Refuse collection
Cleaning services
Any other repair or maintenance costs

If you do not have your own facility but outsource your fulfilment to a fulfilment company, you could record those costs in this section instead. Your list might look like this:

Monthly storage fee
Average monthly picking and dispatch costs
Any other management fees

Staff costs

These include:

Wages
National Insurance
Pension contributions

You may also want to include any HR services you use as a monthly cost if you pay for ongoing support.

Owner salary

One of the biggest issues that I find with product businesses, especially in the early days, is that founders do not consider their salary as part of the cost structure.

When I ran a survey of over 300 small product business owners, the results were staggering. Eighty-one per cent of those surveyed said that they paid themselves either nothing (43%) or less than £1,000 a month from their business.

There is a perception that you have to plough everything back into the business in the early days. And I would certainly say it's very unusual, in the first year at least, for business owners to be paying themselves significantly from their business. After that, if you aren't prioritizing your salary, what are you building the business for?

I often recommend that people read *Profit First* by Michael Micalowiz because he has some real pearls of wisdom when it comes to paying yourself from your business. He states that many people want to grow, and when he asked them why, they said it was because they wanted to pay themselves more from the business. To which his response was, "Why not pay yourself more now?"

He's absolutely right – growth is pointless for us as owners if we can't pay ourselves more. If we don't reward ourselves financially from our businesses, at some point, maybe not in the first year, but eventually, we will lose our ability to keep going.

The other reason why I am passionate about business owners paying themselves from their business is because it does require you to be stricter when it comes to other expenses such as stock; building your discipline when it comes to stock is a crucial skill to develop.

Wherever you are right now in terms of paying yourself, make a start. Make sure that when you work through this break-even analysis, you include something for yourself. Otherwise all you'll calculate is the amount of money that you will need to take in the months you don't pay yourself, and that is not something that you want to plan for.

In terms of how much you should pay yourself from your business, that is a hard question to answer. I would say that if you are paying yourself the equivalent of 25–30% of your turnover then you are doing well – many product business owners are well below that.

As with any financial aspects of your business, I do encourage you to discuss your numbers with your accountant to make sure that you are setting aside the right amount of money for your tax obligations. Effective tax preparation is one of the most important ways to avoid unnecessary stress as a business owner, so make sure you discuss what your obligations are, especially if you generate a significant profit.

Having said that, putting together a break-even analysis will only help you when you sit down to discuss tax planning with your accountant. It's much easier to come prepared with your own figures than to expect them to tell you how your business is doing.

Marketing costs

This section is for you to record all expenses in the business relating to your marketing. For example:

Email marketing software
Social media scheduling software
Printed materials such as flyers
Social media advertising costs
Domain name purchase for website
Website platform, for example Shopify or Squarespace
Website plugins
Any other paid advertising

Other business costs

This is a general bucket for other costs not covered by other categories. Depending on your business, you might want to create other subcategories that make more sense for you, or you may be happy to use this general category.

Here's a list of costs to consider/track:

Accountant
Legal fees such as ongoing legal support
Business mentor or coach
Bank fees
Consultancy/advisory services
Memberships and subscriptions
Stationery and printing
Computers – averaging purchasing costs out across a year
Phone
Internet connection

Travel
Insurance
IT support

Remainder

At the bottom of the break-even analysis, there is a number that shows whether or not the average retail gross profit (RGP) is enough to cover the costs associated with the business.

This is your remainder after fixed costs. A positive remainder shows that your business is in profit based purely on an average month, and a negative remainder shows that you will be running a loss.

The formula is:

$$\text{Remainder} = \text{RGP} - \text{fixed costs}$$

In Irene's case, it shows a positive number. This doesn't necessarily mean that she'll get to keep that money (after all, any profit in a business is taxed), but it does give a sense of whether or not the whole model looks like it works.

Introducing fixed costs

The beauty of this break-even analysis is that once you have it set up, you can model whatever you like in terms of increasing your costs and seeing what impact it has.

You can add them in and then see what you would need to generate in extra sales in order to cover the costs.

Let's say, for example, that Irene is considering taking on an additional staff member. She can put in the additional staff costs and see what impact that would have.

This staff member is going to be full time, and employing them will double Irene's staff costs.

Without changing anything else, she increased the staff costs to £7,000, and now the business is showing that it will be unprofitable in an average month.

Average monthly sales including VAT	£28,000
Excluding VAT	£23,333
Out-margin	60%
Retail gross profit	£14,000
Cost of premises incl utilities	£3,000
Staff costs	£7,000
Owner salary	£2,500
Marketing costs	£3,000
Other business costs	£900
Total costs	£16,400
Remainder	**-£2,400**

She can now play around with the numbers and work out that she'll need to generate another £4,800 worth of sales in order for the whole thing to balance again.

Average monthly sales including VAT	£32,800
Excluding VAT	£27,333
Out-margin	60%

Retail gross profit	£16,400
Cost of premises incl utilities	£3,000
Staff costs	£7,000
Owner salary	£2,500
Marketing costs	£3,000
Other business costs	£900
Total costs	£16,400
Remainder	£0

She'll then need to decide if it feels like the right decision to introduce this extra cost into the business, and if she is confident that she can generate an additional £4,800 a month on average to cover the additional expense.

A word of caution

You need to consider, when it comes to this analysis, that it is based on the idea that you are only spending on stock each month what you need to cover your sales.

Obviously there will be times of the year like Christmas where you end up stockpiling in advance to meet future demand, but it also highlights that you need to make sure that you don't consistently buy more than you sell. Otherwise you will find that your stock is piling up and you are not breaking even, even when it looks like you should.

What if your expenses are driving sales?

One of the trickiest elements of this calculation is looking at what happens if your expenses are actually generating sales for you.

For example, Irene pays a £1,000 retainer each month to an ads specialist, who also spends £2,000 a month on advertising across platforms.

Many business owners I speak to get concerned about these types of expenses, because they feel as if they are not going to be able to cut back on them without losing sales.

The key is to look at how many sales should be coming from that expenditure.

One way to do this quickly is looking at a reverse calculation, using your out-margin and your expenses, to determine how many sales would need to be generated to cover that cost.

If Irene spends a total of £3,000 on the ads specialist across fees and advertising costs, and has a 60% out-margin, she can calculate what the sales need to be to justify that cost.

Sales needed to justify the cost = cost/out-margin + VAT (if VAT registered)

= £3,000/60% + VAT = £5,000 + VAT = £6,000

As long as she is getting at least £6,000 from these ads, she will be breaking even on the ad spend.

The issue that you have with this type of calculation is that it requires you to be able to fully attribute which sales are coming from your ads. Ever since the IOS14 updates in 2021 this has been harder to do.

It still gives you a good sense of what these ads should be driving. For example, if you are spending £3,000 each month, which you know means you have to sell £6,000 in order to break even just from the ads, but your sales are £6,500 and you do lots of other things to generate sales, then it gives you a sense that perhaps you are too reliant on the ads or even that they just aren't generating enough to break even on that expense.

The question you also have to ask yourself is whether you are being, in the words of a former boss, "busy fools". You do have to make sure that you are not spending money to generate sales that themselves have too high a cost associated with them.

It can be a daunting task to consider backing out of an expense that is generating money, but you do have to think about the extent to which you are generating a demand that is costing you money to fulfil.

What if your expenses are too high for your sales?

If you run this analysis and your expenses are too high for your sales, the break-even analysis will show that the minimum sales required to break even are way higher than your current average sales, or you'll see a negative number in the remainder line once you have inputted your average monthly sales.

If that is the case, there are three things you can look at:

1. Play around with the out-margin percentage that you are using for the calculation. The higher the out-margin is, the lower the amount of sales you need to cover your costs. What kinds of margin improvements would you need to make in order to break even? Do you think this is something you can improve?

2. Look at your costs individually. What is it that is driving them up? Have you over-committed in a certain area? Only you will know whether the costs on your fixed-cost list are essential, but it never hurts to take a critical

look and try and identify if there is anything you can cut back.

3. Forecast your sales forward. If you have currently got a good upward sales trajectory (in other words, if you are seeing good improvements over time in your sales month on month or year on year), then you may decide that no action is needed because you feel confident that your business will grow into the size of your current expenses.

The issue here is that if you make this decision, you will want to carefully monitor your sales as time goes by to make sure that you are hitting what you want them to be.

Otherwise you run the risk of being under profitability based on a goal that you didn't hit. That might sound harsh, but at the end of the day I am not averse to setting optimistic goals for the future, as long as you check that your plans do come to pass and make adjustments accordingly if they don't.

Our case studies

Salma the shop owner

This analysis was pretty much what I thought it would be – as I said previously, I do keep a very tight grip on my overheads as they are substantial. I break even based on my average monthly sales, which doesn't surprise me; that's what I thought was happening.

What was fascinating was the impact of the out-margin. I played around with it, and really, just a few percentage-points difference made a big impact on the amount that I needed to sell to cover my costs.

It highlights to me that all the work I am doing to improve my out-margin is well worth it.

Emmanuel the e-commerce seller

It was useful to see how low my sales can dip before I am unable to cover my costs. It helps that my overheads are low.

I also enjoyed being able to map out what my sales would need to look like to double my salary, and to play around with putting in extra costs such as a marketing and admin assistant.

I feel good that I now have this all mapped out. It also helped highlight to me how my margin is causing some real issues. I want to concentrate on improving that before trying to cut back on any more expenses.

Irene the illustrator

While the unit is a big overhead, when I looked at it in comparison to our current sales, it isn't as big of a cost as I had built it up in my head to be.

In my head, all of the profits from the business were being eaten up by the unit. But, looking at this, I can see that it is entirely proportional to the size of the business, which has more than quadrupled in the past three years.

I also played around with the break-even analysis so I can work out exactly how low my sales can go before I'll struggle to cover my costs. I included my salary in that break even as I'm determined to pay myself no matter what.

When I did that, it became clear to me that even in my quietest month in the last two years, I would still have been able to cover the cost of my unit.

I could downsize and find a cheaper unit, but when you factor in all the costs associated with that, I don't think that this makes a lot of sense. I also looked at how the business has been growing over the last couple of years. Even if we grow at half the rate over the next two years, we are totally going to fill, or even outgrow, this unit!

Regardless, I do feel better having the break-even analysis at my fingertips to help guide me when I get stuck, and I feel like I can sleep better knowing this!

Conclusion

Having a break-even calculation is a good way of understanding how much you should be feeding your tiger and gives you a good framework for understanding how your business should be operating.

It also helps you understand how your out-margin can impact your ability to cover your bills, and helps you keep your focus on profitability as a driver.

Of course, one of the elements that can improve the situation for businesses when they are struggling with their break-even calculation is to grow their topline sales, which is what we will explore in Chapter 8.

Key points

- Using a combination of your fixed costs and out-margin, you can see if your average monthly sales are going to be enough to cover your costs.
- If your break-even analysis shows a loss based on your typical monthly sales, it suggests that your business currently has too many expenses, or that your out-margin needs to be higher.

- Once you have this analysis set up, it's easy to update it and use it to model out any changes to your costs, such as adding extra staff members or increasing your salary.
- The break-even analysis is useful to combine with a stock plan as it doesn't work if you are consistently buying more stock each month than you are selling.
- Visit www.resilientretailclub.com/tigertoolkit to get your checklist of costs for the break-even analysis.
- The 'Additional resources' section details further support you can get with the concepts in this chapter.

Over to you

1. Create your own break-even analysis following the format outlined at the start of the chapter. Start with looking at your average monthly sales from the sales plan you completed in Chapter 6, and gather a list of all of your fixed costs in your business using the categories listed at the start of this chapter.

2. Use your out-margin that you calculated in Chapter 4 to work out whether your average sales cover your expenses.

3. How does that feel? Are you surprised by the numbers or is this what you expected?

4. What is the minimum amount of sales in a month that will still cover your costs?

5. What impact would it have if you were to improve your out-margin?

6. What actions are you going to take as a result of this exercise?

CHAPTER 8

WHAT HAVE SALES GOT TO DO WITH IT?

So far in this book, we've walked through all the various elements that make up a tiger's anatomy. Hopefully by now I have convinced you that taming your tiger is less about sales and more about understanding and controlling your profits, stock and other expenses.

However, I didn't feel like I could end the book without a chapter on sales and, more specifically, why not all sales are created equal.

Undoubtedly, when you are looking at your break-even calculation, you can see that there is a level that you need to get to in order to cover your costs. If you're not breaking even, and you can't remove costs or do much to improve your profit margins, you are going to start asking yourself the question as to whether you can improve your sales.

You absolutely need to consider how to grow, and one of the most powerful ways to do so is to both get to grips with your numbers, but also create a strategy for sales growth.

With tools like your master list, product hierarchy, 80/20 analysis, stock plan, sales plan and break-even analysis set up and ready to go, you are in a strong position to grow in a way that doesn't keep you up at night wondering whether you've done the right thing. It will also help you identify potential problems and issues before they even materialize.

When you couple profitable growth with good control of your stock and understanding of your margin, then you are well on your way to a business that feels calmer and more manageable.

In this chapter we are going to look at the elements of a sales plan. Sales growth is often misunderstood by business owners who think that growing your sales always means having more customers. But in fact, there are multiple ways to grow, and some are more profitable than others.

Visit www.resilientretailclub.com/tigertoolkit for resources to help you brainstorm around growing your sales.

Our case studies

Salma the shop owner

I know what sales number I would like to achieve for the shop; I just don't know how to get there. I am also concerned because we are in a physical location with steady footfall. I don't feel like I can magically create hundreds of new local customers. I worry about the best thing to do to drive sales.

Emmanuel the e-commerce seller

I'm always thinking about how to grow, but I've never had a strategic approach before. More often, I get distracted by a "shiny new tactic" without putting together a proper plan. That can mean that I'm often overwhelmed and sometimes feel like I'm running around like a headless chicken.

Irene the illustrator

We've had brilliant growth over the past few years, but even now I'm not 100% sure I could tell you why, hand on my heart.

Of course, there have been several contributing factors to our growth, but sometimes the fact that I can't exactly say what happened makes me nervous. I also worry about our ad costs – we have always done so well with them but in the last six months it feels like it has been much harder work and we've had to fight for every sale.

The four ways to grow sales

Ask most product entrepreneurs what their goals are for their business, and most of them will talk about growing their sales and presence.

When asked for more details, they usually say that they want to get more customers. In other words, they want more people visiting their website, to increase their social media following or see an uplift in orders from their other sales channels.

Did you know that many people are focused primarily on only one method of growing their sales (getting more customers), and are overlooking three others that can make a major difference to the profitability of their business?

The first way to grow sales – getting more customers

Most people think about this method when they look to grow sales. It is what they are aiming their social media efforts at or spending money on advertising to achieve.

The issue with focusing excessively on this method of growth is that it is expensive. Getting more people to come is all about pitching to a cold audience, reaching out to people who have not heard of you before and showing them what you've got to offer.

Getting a steady stream of new traffic onto your site or through your doors should absolutely be a key priority; however, it is expensive and time consuming to constantly be speaking to people who do not know you. It's like hosting a party, but spending all your time trying to persuade more people to join you, instead of focusing on the guests who have already arrived.

There are many ways to get more people to come, and a good sales strategy will incorporate several different methods, including:

- social media marketing;
- PR – getting press coverage for yourself as a business owner and/or for your products;
- paid advertising;
- search engine optimization (SEO) to capture the vast number of online sales that start with a query being typed into a search engine;
- working with content creators/influencers on a gifting or paid basis;
- direct marketing such as flyers;
- collaborating with other brands that share your audience;

- email marketing;
- new sales channels such as marketplaces or wholesale;
- in-person events or pop-ups.

These methods can be time consuming, and slow to yield results, but it's important to have a plan for how you are going to utilize all these different tools over time. Instead, many rely on one tactic, such as social media marketing, and don't look at all of the options available.

The second way to grow sales – getting more people to buy when they do come

Rather than being exclusively focused on getting more fresh leads, a focus on your conversion rate can be far more effective.

If you can improve your conversion rate, your sales will grow without the need for more followers or the need to spend more money on advertising.

Your conversion rate is calculated by taking the number of sales you have in a certain period (for example, the last week or last month) and dividing it by the number of visitors that you had.

Conversion rate = number of transactions/number of visitors expressed as a percentage

So, if you sell two items in a week and have 100 visitors, you have a 2% conversion rate (2/100, expressed as a percentage). This is something that you can calculate easily for a website, or relatively easily for a physical shop.

In a physical shop, you can keep a simple tally chart of the number of people who come into the shop each day (or use a clicker counter) and compare that to the number of sales that you have.

The typical conversion rate for an e-commerce site is around 2%. A physical space will be much higher, with anywhere from 25–50% being typical.

However, you should be comparing yourself not to others, but to what your current conversion rate is. If you can improve that, your sales will increase as you make better use of your existing visitors.

Any time and effort that you spend on improving your online or in-store conversion rate will pay big dividends when it comes to growing your business as it allows you to get more new customers from the people who are already interested rather than spending money and effort to acquire new people.

Improving conversion rates as a topic could probably fill its own book, but my top tips are:

Online:

1. Check the quality of your photography – is it clear and enticing?

2. Check how compelling your product descriptions are. Are you painting a picture for your customers of how much they need your products?

3. Does the customer have all of the information that they need to confidently make a purchase? For example, can they see the back of the item, what's inside it and understand its relative size? Having dimensions on a product page is one thing but, personally, I don't keep a ruler on hand to check what 7cm looks like in real life. A photo with another object for size is so much more useful, or shown on the body if relevant.

4. Do you have an about page that explains who you are and why the business is important to you?

5. How easy is it to make a purchase? How many steps are there between a product page and the checkout? Customers want this stage to be as easy and seamless as possible.

6. Is your website fast enough? Many studies have shown that slower websites negatively impact conversion rates; have you checked how fast your site is?

Offline:

1. Conversion rates in a physical space are often about the service you are offering to your customers. Is each customer being greeted appropriately?

2. Are your best-selling items placed in a prominent place so that customers can easily see them?

3. Is your store layout clear and easy for a customer to follow?

Keep tweaking and refining until you see the conversion rate improving. It's about making more of what you have and refining your business so it's not a leaky bucket.

The other element of conversion that is often overlooked is whether or not you have the products that people want to buy. What we've talked about so far in terms of conversion relates to the technical aspects of online and in-person shopping.

What also helps conversion is when you have desirable products that your customers cannot resist. There are several elements to this.

Probability

What is your customer most likely to want right now? I often think that a huge proportion of retail is about probability. Of everything that you do or could sell, what is the customer most likely to be looking for?

Sometimes that is easy to say because it's all to do with an occasion – if it's early December, chances are they are shopping for Christmas-related items. And if it's early February, it's most likely to be Valentine's. In August and September, for those with stationery or kids brands, back to school is going to be top of the mind.

What about if it's not near any of the main gift-giving occasions? Is it wedding season? Or are people going to be going on holiday? This is all about putting yourself in your customer's shoes and understanding what they are most likely to be interested in right now.

Trial and error

Have a look at the sales that you have generated by product. What is your customer reacting to? What are they telling you that they like? Responding and building on best sellers is definitely a way to drive up your conversion rate because you increase the likelihood that the product on display will be something your customer will like.

Best sellers have a life span – sometimes a couple of years, sometimes 10 years plus! It depends on how "core" the product is. The best time to find a new best seller is when your existing best sellers are still selling well. Retail is about constantly moving forward, not resting on your laurels. As well as allowing you to have a new conversation with your customers, it also helps you stay ahead of potential copycats, too.

Once something is out in the open market, it's fair game. Copying is horrible and unfair, but it happens. Big retailers do it to each other ALL the time. The best way to keep ahead of it is to keep moving forward.

Many big retailers will have testing programmes designed specifically for their key best sellers. They run trials to get a lead on where to take that best seller next. You always want to come up with something that will sell better than your current top seller.

Newness – a key sales stimulator

One of the best ways to create excitement in your business is to have new products to talk about. However, don't be deceived; this does not necessarily mean constantly bringing in a lot of new stock.

Planning 10 or so new launches a year, even of just a few products, can help you grow sales because it is another reason to start a conversation with your customers. If 10 launches sounds completely unachievable for you, consider how you could create new interest with a minimal stock investment.

Could you, for example, bring in a new colour of one product? How about a collaboration with another brand? Or purchase a small number of products from another business that complement your existing range and tell your customers about that.

Scarcity

One of the biggest drivers of purchasing can be a perception of scarcity. I don't believe in false scarcity (where you make false claims about how few you have left), but in general, you want your demand to be slightly ahead of your supply.

Getting to the point where your customer knows that they can come back any time and purchase from you is going to make it harder to sell things immediately.

The third way to grow sales – getting each customer to spend more

Instead of focusing on getting more new customers, another way to drive sales that is often overlooked is measuring and increasing the ATV, or average transaction value, also known as your average basket size.

This is a very profitable way to grow as it requires no additional customers or marketing.

ATV = total sales value of your orders/number of orders placed

For example, your sales were £300 across five orders.

Your ATV is £300/5 = £60.

If you can increase the amount spent by each customer to £66, your sales will increase by 10% without the need to get any more customers than you already have.

Monitoring your ATV on a monthly basis will help you track how you are moving this number forward.

Ways to increase your ATV include:

Mix of items

If you are mostly selling lower-priced items, can you promote more of your higher-priced items in your marketing and social media to encourage customers to buy those instead? Do you even have any higher-priced items to offer your customers? Can you trial some higher price points to see what happens?

Bundles

Increasing your number of gift sets or putting products together into bundles at a small discount (e.g. total price is £35, you offer it at £32). This increases the average amount of money spent by each customer.

Additional items

You often see add-on items online under the "You may also like" feature. In a shop, these will be the till-point add-on purchases. Big retailers put a lot of time and effort into working out the best products to put on and near tills to encourage impulse buying, because they understand the power of increasing their ATV. Even £1 extra being spent by a customer across an entire business can have a dramatic impact.

Free shipping

Sometimes you can play around with offers like free shipping to encourage an increase in your ATV. Don't set a limit that is way above your ATV; look for one that is around 10% higher, so that customers that get close are tempted to increase the size of their order.

If you know that your customer spends £45 on average, try offering free shipping over £50. It may encourage that extra purchase to push them over the limit. If you are in a physical store, consider offering something like free gift wrapping over a certain purchase.

As with your conversion rate, keep trying new ways to boost your ATV, and check it each month to see how you are progressing.

The fourth way to grow sales – getting existing customers to buy more often

The final method to grow your sales is to get your existing customers to buy more often, or how you nurture your customers to keep them engaged.

Are you reaching out to people who have bought from you previously to see how they felt about your products? Are you encouraging them to buy again or to take a look at your new products?

You have a much higher chance of converting a previous customer than converting someone who is coming across your brand for the first time.

One of my favourite sayings is "no-one is more likely to buy from you than someone who has already bought from you", and it's something worth bearing in mind throughout your whole business journey.

What are you doing to reach out and ask for the next sale? This is where email marketing is important. Are you tagging customers when they make a potentially recurring purchase, such as a yearly diary, so that you can target them with a follow-up?

Do you know who your VIP/most frequent customers are? These are the most important group of customers you have. Do you have a special loyalty scheme for them? Ultimately, these are the people who pay your bills, so why not take 10 minutes to brainstorm how you can keep them happy?

Repeat customers are generally much better customers all round. They tend to return fewer items, spend more and are much more likely to complete reviews or feedback and advocate for your brand. They are well worth your time and attention.

Monitoring

The most important part of growing your sales is to keep an eye on all of these four elements on a monthly basis. Keep trying and tweaking your offering until you see an improvement.

In the case of your repeat customers, keep trying different email marketing approaches to encourage repeat purchases. Keep monitoring who your VIPs are and working on ways to make them happy.

Some of the key statistics that are useful to add to a monthly business review are the following:

- conversion rate;
- average order value;
- visitor numbers;
- bounce rate (for websites);
- return visitor percentage (for websites).

Tracking these numbers means that as you try new strategies, you can start to see what is happening and what difference they are making.

Our case studies

Salma the shop owner

Looking at the different ways to grow revenue made me think about how I've been approaching my sales. Our POS system does allow us to track by customer, and it's become obvious that a big percentage of our sales are coming from a group of loyal customers.

I decided to reach out to each one individually, not particularly with a sales pitch, but more to say hi and see how they are doing. So many people were touched to hear from me, and we had quite a few coming along and popping in as we'd reminded them that we were here!

Looking at the different ways that we've been driving sales, I decided to track our in-store conversion rate. We bought a little clicker counter like the kind they use to count people in at concerts and started tracking how many people were coming into the shop compared to the number of transactions on the till. What I noticed was that when I was in the shop, the conversion rate was on average about 25% higher than when it was my team members on their own.

I decided to get them together to talk about this, and I found that many of them felt awkward approaching customers who were just browsing.

We came up with a list of best practices – a friendly smile, stopping any tasks we are doing to say hello and, after a certain amount of time, asking if they were looking for something in particular. This chat also highlighted that there was a variety of different levels of confidence amongst the team when it came to making suggestions, so I gave each member the task of coming up with three great gift ideas according to who the person was buying for.

I kept tracking the conversion rates, and we started to see small improvements during the times where the team was there alone. I also noticed that several of them seemed much more engaged, and I even got a lovely card from a customer who was impressed with the help they got from one of my staff when they were feeling stuck with what to buy as a gift.

There's still lots to think about, but I'm pleased with how we've been able to grow our sales in our shop, with no extra footfall or marketing needed. I never would have focused on this issue if it hadn't been for measuring the conversion rate.

Emmanuel the e-commerce seller

I decided to take a look at all four areas of growing sales and work through what actions I am going to take for each.

Getting more people to come – I wanted to delve into this some more and look at how the people who are coming to my website are generating sales. I set up Google Analytics; I can't believe I haven't done that before, and best of all, it's free!

Firstly, the majority of my traffic was coming from social media, which I was quite pleased about until I saw exactly how bad the conversion rate was. Overall, I'm at 1.9%, which is under the industry average, slightly, but OK. However, the social media conversion rate was only 1%.

Organic traffic doesn't amount to much, but I was able to see that the most commonly used search term to find my website was "stainless steel tumblers" and my most visited page was my blog post on eco-friendly picnics that featured the tumblers.

I feel like search engine optimization (SEO) is a great place for me to spend some focus – that traffic was converting at well over 3%, so clearly a beneficial use of my time.

I also could see that a fair amount of traffic was coming from an article on the "top 5 best wine glasses for your home" from the website of a monthly women's magazine. I'd totally forgotten about that piece and I was amazed to see that 12 months later it is still pumping traffic my way. Definitely something to keep in mind and focus on getting more PR coverage.

Conversion rate – as I said, it's a bit below average but not horrible. The only thing that worries me is the fact that it has dropped over time. Conversion rates were lower than last year so I'm having a look at specific pages with low conversion rates as well as checking my mobile site speed.

Getting people to spend more – I guess that I already do multibuy offers to drive up the average selling price of my products, so I felt comfortable with that.

I did look at creating some higher-priced bundles. I put together a "perfect picnic" hamper with everything for eating outside for two – blanket, tumblers, picnic plates with the carry-bag – and I sold one the first week I listed it! I don't imagine that I'll sell massive volumes but it generates a decent amount of money. I will continue watching and thinking about my sales for more ideas.

Irene the illustrator

For me, this exercise helped me think a lot about my most loyal customers. There are people who have whole kitchens kitted out with our ceramics and prints, and they are always the ones who are posting excitedly about my latest release on social media.

I wanted to look at how to take care of them better. I am looking into a loyalty programme, but to start off with, I looked at my email marketing software, which has the ability to segment according to how many times people have bought from me. I was able to send out a thank you coupon, only a small discount, to my most loyal customers and I was so touched by how people responded. I felt like they were so happy to hear from me and appreciated enormously that I was recognizing their loyalty.

I want to spend more time going forward working with my most loyal customers. I asked a few of them what they wanted to get from me and they showed an interest in more access, and more ability to give their input into products and new designs.

I also took a look at our average order value, which was enlightening. I definitely have seen it drop since we launched our mugs. They are so popular and that's great, but it's £10 instead of £29 for a print and so I do think we've seen a drop. I have set our free shipping limit at £35 now, so 10% above our current average order value (roughly), and that seems, from early indications, to be having an impact.

I also looked at an upselling app that is making suggestions to people at checkout and even though only one in 10 people are purchasing from it, when I look at the extra money that has been generated, it's encouraging.

Conclusion

As your sales numbers grow, things can get more complicated. Don't make the mistake of thinking that all you need to do to tame your tiger is to sell more.

However, a well-thought-out sales strategy coupled with a strong understanding of your key numbers is important when it comes to growing your business in a way that feels controlled.

Successful product businesses do not just measure how many new customers they are getting each month; they focus on growing sales through all four areas. If you do the same, you will not only increase your topline sales, but your profits will grow too.

You may also find that having a broad range of strategies to grow your sales will help, over time, create more consistent sales for your business. If you are solely reliant on one tactic, such as social media, to bring in new customers, then if you have issues with that platform it can impact your whole business. Diversified ways of growing sales can help even out the highs and lows.

Creating a business that is growing profitably is about much more than trying to get more people through the door or onto the website. It's about creating a sales strategy that takes into consideration all of the different ways to grow.

Remember your break-even analysis from Chapter 7? Certain elements of growing your sales are going to require external support or extra investment. Keep reviewing that analysis to make sure that any extra expenses you take on have a clear sales number that they need to generate to be profit-positive.

Profitable sales growth often depends on growing using the second, third and fourth methods. That's because improving your conversion rates, encouraging customers to spend more in each transaction and nurturing your existing customers are all much, much cheaper than spending the money to get brand-new cold leads through your doors.

Now that we've explored the importance of sales, it's time to consider how all of the elements of being a tiger tamer can be incorporated into your month-to-month activities as a business owner.

Key points

- There are four ways to grow your sales:
    - get more people to come;
    - get more people to buy when they do come;
    - get people to spend more;
    - get people to come back more often.
- A good sales strategy will cover all of these methods and will help you, over time, build more consistent sales.
- For any cost associated with driving sales, it's worth checking what additional sales you will need to make that worthwhile.

- Visit www.resilientretailclub.com/toolkit for materials to help you brainstorm your sales growth across the four types of sales.

Over to you

1. How do you currently get sales to your website? Use Google Analytics or your own website analytics to understand:

   a. Where are the sales coming from?

   b. What are the conversion rates coming from?

   c. How would you like to drive more sales?

   d. If there's a cost attached, make sure you can run the break-even calculation from Chapter 6 to help you understand what sales you need to generate to cover that cost.

2. If you have a physical location, consider implementing a simple question, "Where did you hear about us?", to customers coming in; perhaps keep a simple tally chart by the till of what the answer was. Understanding on where sales are coming from can help.

3. Look at your conversion rate. What can you try to improve?

4. Look at your average order value. What could be an option there?

5. Think about your best customers:

   a. What are you doing to help them?

   b. What more can you do?

   c. Referrals and word-of-mouth support are crucial; what can you do to get more of those?

CHAPTER 9

BECOMING A TIGER TAMER

Congratulations on reaching the final chapter! You've taken the time and effort needed to understand more about how product businesses make money and how to make them into tame, friendly tigers instead of ravenous beasts.

We've examined the bite – looking at the top teeth (in-margin) and bottom teeth (out-margin) as well as the tail and the stomach.

You may even have started to look at the numbers as they relate to your own business, and hopefully will have developed a sense of how useful key figures are in helping you understand and make decisions about your business.

The question I'd like to ask you now is, how are you going to integrate what you have learnt back into your business?

After all, we are all busy, with endless to-do lists, so how do you carve out time to look at these figures?

This is a great point for you to go to www.resilientretailclub. com/tigertoolkit to get your checklist for an effective monthly review.

I'd like to offer a couple of alternatives. The first is what I would call the "if you do nothing else" approach – this is the approach outlined in Appendix 1 and is a great option if you are feeling overwhelmed at the prospect of running through everything in the book. The second is the monthly review.

Monthly review

While the "if you do nothing else" approach will still give you a lot of insight into your business, the ideal situation is making the time once a month for a "tiger tamer" session, where you review your numbers and make decisions on how to move forward.

This monthly review will help you deepen your understanding of your business and make smarter, more focused decisions. Over time, you'll also learn to recognize and avoid problems long before they develop, as well as keeping your stock in a healthy place.

A thorough review will incorporate the following seven tasks:

A sales review

Were the sales for the month above or below the plan that you set? What drove your sales? Where were they coming from, and which of your sales channels was the most effective this month?

Look at Chapter 8 and see if you can pinpoint which method of driving sales has been the most effective. It's also a good opportunity to review key sales statistics such as conversion rate and average transaction value to monitor how they are shifting month on month.

Check your in-margin

Do you have any new products that you are bringing in? These should be checked before you agree to buy anything, but it's worth putting in time once a month to do a round-up in case you bought any quickly that were not fully checked first.

It's also a good idea to double check any invoices you had coming in the last month – whether that was your packaging or anything else – to make sure that costs are not creeping up and that your master sheet is still up to date. See Chapter 3 for more details.

Check your out-margin

Pull the sales data out of your systems and run your out-margin calculation based on what you sold. Review Chapter 4 for more details on how to do this.

It's important to run this number every month to make sure it isn't dipping or shifting too far down. Hopefully, if you have started paying close attention to your discounting, you should see it creeping up.

If it has dropped, do you know why? Perhaps you have been running a stock clearance sale, which is all well and good, as we discussed previously these are necessary. I would be interested to understand why the out-margin had dropped so that it is a clear, strategic decision instead of simply noting that it has dropped.

Look ahead at the month coming up – what levels of discounting do you expect? Do you want to cancel or remove a discount from the plan or reduce it?

Run your 80/20 analysis, best sellers, worst sellers and any other analysis that is relevant.

Get clarity on how much stock you have in the business; take the time to analyse what is and is not working. See Chapter 5 for more information on how to complete these analyses.

Most importantly, make sure you are making a list of actions to take once you have completed that analysis. There is no point running numbers for the sake of it. Ask yourself what these figures are telling you, and what you are going to do about them.

For example, do you have a sale coming up in the near future? Have you already started to identify what it is that you want to put into the sale to clear it out? What are these numbers telling you about the stock you are planning to buy; are you still happy that you are making the right decision?

Review your stock plan

Are you over or under your plan for your stock? How does it compare to what you are forecasting? Look at Chapter 6 for more information on creating and maintaining your plan.

If you've got too much stock, what can you do to sell more or to reduce the amount that you have coming in? How do you clear back stock? What actions can you take to reduce it?

If you are below your stock plan, what can you do to improve that? Can you place larger orders or otherwise find ways to get more stock in more quickly?

Review your break-even analysis

For more information on a break-even analysis, review Chapter 7. Each month, you should review your expenses compared to what you have mapped out on your break-even analysis. Is there anything unexpected that you had previously not included? Is your out-margin the same or different to your plan?

What does your plan and your current performance tell you in terms of what you need to do to keep the business on the right track? Are there any changes you need to make or issues you need to be aware of?

Look forward

How are your sales plans looking for the next few months? Does it all look right to you or do you need to adjust? If they have been consistently under or over performing, does this suggest that you need to rework your plans?

If sales aren't coming in the way you want, do you understand why? What is not working as you expect? If sales are coming in better than expected, what is driving that?

Most importantly, do you need to make any business decisions based on the plan? Do you need to make any changes to your plans for the next couple of months, whether that's around your stock buying, your promotional plans or product launches? Take some time to make a list of actions to help you stay focused on what needs to happen.

Completing these seven tasks will help you feel in the driving seat. Instead of feeling lost or confused as to where your money has gone, you are able instead to take a look at the figures on an ongoing basis. Checking in on what has happened during that month will give you the opportunity to have a good handle on where you are compared to your plans, and to anticipate or even avoid potential problems.

Our case studies

Salma the shop owner

When I think about where I was before I started this process, I think that the difference has been quite staggering. I have gone from feeling lost and on the back foot to being much more clued in.

Each month, I have a day where I take myself and my laptop out of the shop and into the local coffee shop for a "CEO day". I run through the sales figures (it got much quicker than it was the first time I did it!), look at where I performed against the previous month, check my out-margin and look at my best and worst sellers.

I then look over my buying plans for the next couple of months and run through the products I'm planning on ordering. I check the category mix and how I'm planning on buying. I look at how much stock I have left of similar items. I also take a look at my slowest categories and think about whether or not I want to promote any of those to clear them out, or mark them as not to be reordered so I know I want to run down the stock I have of them.

Having an idea of how much stock I have and how to best work with it has been transformative for me and my business. Not to mention understanding the impact that my profit margin was having on my ability to cover my costs.

My break-even analysis has also helped me focus on what everything needs to be in order to work.

Once I had all my templates set up, it doesn't take me too long to pull the numbers once a month. I feel more relaxed and confident. It doesn't stop me worrying about the slow days – after all, I am human – but knowing where to start looking has helped me.

Emmanuel the e-commerce seller

At first I was sceptical about taking the time to work through all of these numbers every month. I barely feel like I have enough time during the day as it is. However, I was pleasantly surprised at how quickly I was able to create my Tiger Tamer's Toolkit and how useful it was.

As my out-margin has been a big focus for me, I always make sure to run that first. I have seen an improvement and I'm able to see how my profits have been increasing even when my sales have stayed level. The business feels a lot less frantic, and I'm happy to see my hard work paying off.

After the realization that so much of my stock was in the tail, I have decided to not actively discount most stuff to clear it, but to avoid reordering and just sell out. I can see how the big shipments from the supplier are messing up my stock numbers, but I don't see a way around it. At least I can foresee what my stock holding will be and it doesn't feel like it's such a surprise.

Overall, I'd say that running these numbers hasn't exactly felt great – I definitely feel like I had to look at some hard truths squarely in the face. Now that I've done that, I feel like I have genuine direction on where to take the business to keep it moving forward in the way that I want to.

More than anything, I have got to grips with the relationship between what's in my bank account compared to what is on my shelves. It's clear to me that the quicker I turn my stock, the more money I will have, and the better margins I achieve when I sell my stock, the more likely I am to be able to grow profitably.

Irene the illustrator

I feel like I might be turning into a numbers geek after all! Now that I know where to look and what I'm supposed to be focusing on, I find it satisfying to analyse my numbers.

That said, after a lot of thinking, I've asked one of my team members to help me out with numbers. At first, I felt awkward giving someone else in the business the same kind of visibility that I have, but we had a good chat about confidentiality. She totally understood the importance of not sharing the information with everyone – not that I'm trying to be overly secretive but it made me feel more comfortable.

Once a month, we sit down together and she runs me through the best and worst sellers, as well as where our out-margin is coming in.

She also runs all of the margin figures for me so that as we're developing new products, we can make a decision on whether or not the margins are right. She's also started updating everything with the new pricing as we get invoices in so we can always see what is going on.

I think for me, what this exercise has done is giving me a much better understanding of how the business is running, and also the kinds of costs that we can and can't support. We were discussing bringing in some more packing help and I was able to run it through the break-even analysis to help me feel comfortable that we could afford it. I've also started paying myself more out of the business based on what I can see the sales can support.

After looking at the stock figures in particular, I walked around the unit and looked at how much space was being taken up by unproductive stock. Although I don't feel like our stock holding is completely out of hand in relation to our sales, I can see ways in which it could be lower and also avoid the need for us to add in a mezzanine, just yet!

We started doing some specific targeted discounts on some of the underperforming stock, and clearing that out has made a big difference to the amount of room we had. We also had so many bits and pieces that were taking up space in the racking that we decided to do a seconds and sample sale. It was brilliant – we did it as a live event which got people excited, and our team all took part. Clearing out those old bits of stock made a big difference and helped with a nice bit of extra cash flow!

Now I feel like I not only have a plan for the next few months; I'll know what I need to do and what I need to look at in order to make adjustments if things don't go as planned.

Conclusion

With this book, you have the tools and methods in place to review and understand your business and, more importantly, what will make you money.

Ultimately, a little knowledge you develop is better than none, and any discipline you develop now around your numbers will help enormously as you grow.

Key points

- Taming your tiger requires a regular monthly slot to review your data.
- Finding the time to do your "CEO" work will give you a much better view of what is happening.
- Ask yourself the following questions:
  - What were my sales vs. plan and last year?
  - What was my out-margin?
  - What were my best sellers and what were they telling me?
  - What were my worst sellers and what were they telling me?

- ◆ How much stock do I have?
- ◆ How is that stock split between productive and non-productive stock?
- ◆ What actions do I need to take?
- Taking the time to look at this information and ask these questions on a regular basis will help you feel more confident and in control of your business.
- If you go to www.resilientretailclub.com/tigertoolkit, you can get a checklist on creating an effective monthly review for your business.
- The 'Additional resources' section details further support you can get with the concepts in this chapter.

Over to you

1. Go to www.resilientretailclub.com/tigertoolkit and download your Tiger Tamer's Toolkit to take advantage of all of the free bonus resources that come with the book, including a checklist on an effective monthly review.

2. Start gathering the elements that you need to complete it and put some time into your diary to get your templates set up the way you need them for your business.

3. Find a date in your diary for a CEO day to make some time to work through the analysis from the previous month.

4. Work through the questions list and put together some plans to move forward.

5. Take a few moments to reflect – how does your business feel now you have the tools to more effectively analyse what is happening?

6. What are you going to do now? Where are you going to start? While you are thinking about it, why not get out a notepad and make a list of actions to take right now vs. ones that you can take later on?

FINAL THOUGHTS

Thank you so much for taking the time to read this book and engage with the concepts and ideas. In writing this book, my biggest goal was to reach out to and support as many product business owners as possible.

I really hope you now feel empowered to look at your business in a new way. If it feels overwhelming, just start small. Focus on one thing at first, or look at 'Appendix 1: If you do nothing else' to see the small, but powerful, steps you can take to deepen your understanding and improve how you relate to your business.

Remember that there *is* a way to tame your tiger. You can understand how your sales, profits and expenses align. You don't have to feel baffled by where your money is going. The answers are all there, and now you know where to look.

ADDITIONAL RESOURCES

1. Don't miss out on the free resource bundle that complements this book – get your toolkit at www. resilientretailclub.com/tigertoolkit

    The toolkit contains helpful bonus material to support you with each chapter of the book, from margins and checklists, to prompts to help you brainstorm ways to grow your sales.

2. I offer lots of other free resources, including my podcast The Resilient Retail Game Plan – find out more at www. resilientretailclub.com

3. I would love to invite you to join The Resilient Retail Club at www.resilientretailclub.com/membership

    Are you more of a visual learner? Inside the Club you will find an in-depth Tiger Tamer course with videos, templates and exercises designed to walk you through the concepts in this book in greater detail. Many people have shared how actually watching something on screen and having pre-made templates is enormously beneficial to them.

    Although the book is designed to allow you to complete all of the exercises you need to understand your business just from the information set out in these pages, the course is a shortcut to getting to grips with your key numbers and goes into more detail than it is possible to do with the written word alone.

    The course gives you:

    - an in-depth tutorial on calculating your in-margin;
    - videos and templates to create a master list and an out-margin analysis;

- the template and explainer videos for the 80/20 analysis;
- template and in-depth tutorial for creating a stock plan;
- a break-even analysis template and instructions;
- detailed breakdown of the four types of sales growth;
- a template for a monthly review.

There are also hundreds of other businesses in the Club who are ready to cheer you on and help you stay accountable within our private community. Plus, we also have a whole range of other courses available for members and four live workshops or talks a month. All this for a low monthly fee and no minimum sign-up.

4. Finally, why not hire me to help you tame your tiger?

I work with a number of established brands each year to help them tame their tiger and build their business profitably. Find out more at www.resilientretailclub.com

GET IN TOUCH

As a small business owner, I'm sure you know exactly how important reviews are. So, if you enjoyed this book, it would mean so much to me if you would take the time to review it and share.

Got any thoughts or questions after reading the book? You can tag or message me on @resilientretailclub on Instagram, TikTok and Facebook, and also on LinkedIn at www.linkedin.com/in/catherineerdly

FURTHER READING

How to be a Productivity Ninja - Graham Allcott
If you ever struggle with time management, this is an indepth look at maximizing efficiency.

7 Habits of Highly Effective People - Stephen R. Covey
A classic, for good reason. It will give you a new perspective on life and business.

The Mom Test - Rob Fitzpatrick
If you've ever struggled to get meaningful customer feedback, this is a great book to help you ask the right questions.

Superfans - Pat Flynn
A useful way to understand how to create and keep fans of your brand.

Profit First - Mike Micalowiz
A powerful new way to look at your business and a firm advocate for building a business that pays you!

You Are a Badass - Jen Sincero
My personal favourite to help keep you motivated - the audio version is particularly good.

Watertight Marketing - Bryony Thomas
A very practical book on how to evaluate and improve your marketing efforts.

Hype Yourself - Lucy Werner
The ultimate guide to self-promotion for small business owners.

For more small business resources, I highly recommend visiting Small Business Britain at https://smallbusinessbritain.uk and Enterprise Nation www.enterprisenation.com for their wealth of information.

APPENDIX 1:
IF YOU DO NOTHING ELSE

These are the elements that I consider to be the bare minimum to feel comfortable and less stressed out by your tiger.

Check your margins

Even if creating the analysis for your out-margin (see Chapter 4 for more detail on out-margins) feels too time consuming, you must check your in-margins to make sure that you are making money on your sales. (See Chapter 3 for more details on in-margin analysis.) At the absolute bare minimum, before agreeing to sell something through your business, make sure it is making 50% margin when bought in from another business, and if you intend to sell it on via wholesale, it will need to be at least 65–70% margin.

Most importantly, know what your current average in-margin is and keep looking at ways to improve that. Don't forget to keep these numbers up to date as prices increase – I suggest updating your profit margins at least once a quarter.

Know your break even

In my experience, having a strong understanding of what sales are required to cover your fixed costs, based on your out-margin and your average sales, is one of the most powerful numbers you can know as a business owner. Even if you have to do it based on an estimate of your out-margin, work it through using the format we explored in Chapter 7 so that you have that break-even number firmly in your mind.

Watch your stock

If the only thing that you recall from this entire book is the phrase "the bigger the tail, the bigger the tiger", then I'll be satisfied. Too much stock and underproductive stock creating pockets of trapped cash is one of the most dangerous things that can happen to a product business.

Knowing, at the absolutely bare minimum, how much stock you have and avoiding it piling up is crucial. If this is your focus, refer to Chapters 5 and 6 for more detail.

APPENDIX 2:
LIST OF FORMULAS USED

Chapter 3 – The top teeth

In-margin (non-VAT-registered businesses) = (selling price – total product costs)/selling price × 100

In-margin (20% VAT-registered businesses) = ((selling price/1.2) – total product costs)/(selling price/1.2) × 100

Target cost price (non-VAT-registered businesses) = retail price × (1 – ideal margin)

Target cost price (20% VAT-registered businesses) = (retail price/1.2) × (1 – ideal margin)

Chapter 4 – The bottom teeth

Out-margin (non-VAT-registered businesses) = (total sales – total product costs including packaging – selling fees – postage)/total sales × 100

Out-margin (20% VAT-registered businesses) = ((total sales/1.2) – total product costs including packaging – selling fees – postage)/(total sales/1.2) × 100

=VLOOKUP(A2,Master List !A:H,8,false)

Where A2 is the location of the item you want to look up, Master List!A:H is the location of the sales data, 8 is the number of columns you want to count over and false indicates that you only want to see a perfect match.

Chapter 5 – Understanding the size of your tiger's tail

Cover = stock/average weekly sales

Chapter 6 – The tail

Number of weeks' cover = total amount of stock/average weekly sales

Ideal closing stock = desired weeks' cover × average weekly sales

Amount available to spend = ideal closing stock – (this month's opening stock – the sales plan for the month – the discount amount + any confirmed intake)

Actual closing stock = opening stock – sales – discounts + confirmed intake + amount available to spend

Chapter 7 – The stomach

Retail gross profit = sales (excl. VAT) × out-margin

Remainder = RGP – fixed costs

Sales needed to justify the cost = cost/out-margin + VAT (if VAT registered)

Chapter 8 – What have sales got to do with it?

Conversion rate = number of transactions/number of visitors expressed as a percentage

ATV (average transaction value) = total sales value of your orders/number of orders placed

APPENDIX 3: GLOSSARY OF TERMS

80/20 rule – also known as the Pareto principle, the 80/20 rule describes how 80% of results are usually achieved by 20% of effort, or in the case of product businesses, how 80% of sales usually come from 20% of products. See Chapter 5 for more details.

Add-on purchase – an additional item, often purchased at the point of checkout. For example, buying shoe polish with a pair of shoes.

ATV – average transaction value.

Autumn/Winter (AW) – used to reference a selling season for products.

Average order value (AOV) – the same as ATV.

Average selling price – the total sales value divided by the number of units sold. Allows you to understand whether your higher-priced or lower-priced products are selling more.

B2B – business-to-business.

B2C – business-to-customer.

Back to school – sometimes abbreviated to BTS – peak selling period in August/September for anything related to school supplies or clothes.

Backend – the part of a website or system that is not visible to the customer.

Backorder – when a product is sold out, it might be put on backorder and sent at a later point when it arrives back in stock.

Basket size – the average amount of money spent by a customer per transaction. Another name for ATV/AOV.

Best seller – a product in your business that generates significant sales compared to the rest of your range.

Blanket discount – offering money off everything in your business. "25% off everything today only" is a blanket discount.

Bottom line – another word for your business profit.

Bounce rate – the percentage of people who leave your website after viewing only a single page. Lower is better.

Break-even point – the amount of sales you have to generate to cover all of your costs in your business.

Bricks and clicks – a business with both a physical location and also a website.

Bricks and mortar – a physical shop.

Business rates – UK taxes charged to non-domestic premises such as shops.

Carriage paid – a term used when selling wholesale that refers to a set amount where, if reached, the supplier offers free postage.

Cash flow – the amount of money that goes in and comes out of a company. Whereas profit might be measured over a set period of time such as the financial year, cash flow has to be monitored constantly as the timing of the money coming in and going out is crucial to maintaining a positive cash flow where you have money in the bank.

Cash poor – a business that struggles to have enough cash flow to cover bills and expenses.

Cash rich – a business where there is enough cash in the business bank account to easily cover expenses and invest in new products or support.

Category analysis – a piece of analysis that examines your sales broken down by the different categories of stock. For example, looking at how T-shirts are selling compared to sweatshirts. See Chapter 5 for more information.

Clearance sale – a promotional event in your business where the main focus is on clearing out stock to bring in more cash. Discounts tend to be quite substantial to encourage customers to buy.

Closing stock – the amount of stock you have in your business at the end of a time period, such as the end of a month.

Commission – a percentage of your sales that is taken out before you receive the proceeds. For example, a marketplace might take 20% commission on your products it sells through their site.

Commitment – another word for orders you have placed with suppliers that have not yet been received by you.

Confirmed intake – another word for commitment (see above).

Container – usually refers to a shipping container when referring to products being shipped from overseas.

Conversion rate – the number of people buying from you compared to the number of people who visited your website or store, as a percentage.

Cost price (CP) – the cost that you pay to your supplier for a product.

Cover – a theoretical number that shows you how many weeks' worth of stock you would have if you continued to sell at the same rate that you are currently selling at. For example, if you have 50 lampshades and you sell on average five a week, then you have 10 weeks' worth of stock left.

Cross-costing – the process of getting a quote from more than one supplier for the same product, to allow you to compare them.

DC – distribution centre.

Discontinued – used if a product is not going to be restocked.

Discount – any time you offer a price reduction to your customer.

Drop shipping – the process where products are listed for sale on a website, and only physically dispatched from the manufacturer once a sale has taken place.

Duty – usually refers to import duty, which are several different taxes due on goods purchased from abroad.

Email marketing – the use of email marketing software to communicate with multiple customers. It may include a regular newsletter as well as other specific types of emails such as welcome emails or reminders to customers who leave your site without purchasing.

End of line – when you have just a few items left of a product you do not intend to restock.

Etsy – international marketplace with thousands of sellers.

Ex VAT – short for excluding VAT.

Fixed costs – anything that relates to the business that doesn't typically change month to month as sales fluctuate. Rent and utility bills are examples of fixed costs.

Flash sale – a promotional event that is often run for a short period of time, such as 24 hours.

Footfall – the number of people entering a shop or shopping area at a particular time.

Forecast – a prediction or estimate of future sales.

Free postage or free shipping – when you cover the cost of postage for your customer. You will need to pay for it, but they do not see it as an additional cost at the end of the checkout journey. Often used as a way to incentivize a purchase or entice customers to increase the amount they are spending. For example, offering free postage over £50.

Fulfilment centre – a distribution centre run by a third party that will store your stock and send it out to your customers on your behalf.

Fulfilment costs – the money you pay the fulfilment centre to store you stock and dispatch it.

Gross profit – sales minus VAT and product costs, also known as RGP or retail gross profit.

Gross sales – total sales before taxes.

Gross selling price – the selling price of an item including VAT.

Import duty – different taxes due on goods purchased from abroad.

Inc VAT – short for including VAT.

In-margin – what you buy an item for compared to what you are planning on selling it at. See Chapter 3 for more details.

Introductory offer – a discount used to entice customers to place their first order or sign up to a mailing list. For example, "10% off your first order when you sign up to my newsletter" is an introductory offer.

Inventory – stock.

Lead magnet – something you give away in return for email sign-ups.

Lead time – the time it will take to send and deliver an order.

Living wage – a wage that is high enough to maintain a normal standard of living.

Mailing list – the list that you maintain of names and email addresses that you have permission to send marketing communications to.

Manufacturer – a person or company that makes goods for you to sell.

Manufacturing run – a continuous period of producing a product, also known as a production run.

Margin – usually refers to your profit margin.

Master list – also referred to as a range plan. It is a record, in a spreadsheet, of every item that you sell, along with some key information about each one.

Minimum order – the minimum amount you have to spend per order from a supplier.

Minimum order quantity (MOQ) – the minimum buy quantity of one product.

Multibuy – a type of discount where you have to buy a certain number of items to get it. three for two is a multibuy.

Net profit – gross profit minus fixed costs.

Net sales – gross sales minus VAT.

Net selling price – gross selling price minus VAT.

Occasion – a gift-giving event such as Valentine's Day or Mother's Day.

Open to buy (OTB) – the amount you can spend on stock during a certain period.

Opening stock – the amount of stock you have at the beginning of a time period, such as a month.

Out of stock (OOS) – sold out but usually used if the item will be coming back into stock.

Out-margin – an analysis of historical sales data to show what profit margin you actually achieved during a set time period.

Overheads – also known as fixed costs.

Packaging – the materials used to send a product to the customer.

Pareto principle – see the 80/20 rule.

PDF – portable document format, a type of file that is easy to send via email.

Pick – an order fulfilment process where items from a customer order are retrieved from their location in a fulfilment centre such as on a shelf.

Point of sale (POS) – something that will help sell the brand; often it's a sign with the story of the brand or a display unit for the range with some branding.

Point of sale system (POS system) – (not the same as the POS above), usually the till and stock management system all in one.

Pop-up – a temporary shop.

Postage – the cost of sending an item to a customer.

Postage and packing (P&P) – the term for the amount charged to the customer to cover the costs of sending an item.

PR – public relations. For small businesses this usually refers to the process of getting your products (or you as the business owner) featured in the press.

Product attribute – a feature of a product such as its colour or size.

Product category – a classification such as "Cards" or "Kitchen goods" that help you break down your sales data in a more meaningful way.

Product costs – the costs associated with creating or buying a product. These will fluctuate – the more you sell, the higher the product costs will be.

Product hierarchy – a way of organizing your products into categories and subcategories.

Product mix – the total range of products offered by a business.

Product testing – testing is done to make sure a product meets all legal requirements and is labelled with all the relevant warning labels.

Profit – the amount of money remaining after all expenses have been taken into account.

Profit margin – the profit expressed as a percentage of the net selling price.

Profitability – the degree to which your business generates profit.

Range plan – a record, in a spreadsheet, of every item that you sell, along with some key information about each one.

Raw materials – the basic elements that go into making up your product.

Recommended retail price (RRP) – the price the supplier recommends that your product should be sold at.

Reorder – to repurchase an item that you currently sell.

Repeat customer – someone buying from you not for the first time.

Retail – selling products to the end customer as opposed to wholesale. Can be online or in person.

Retail gross profit (RGP) – sales minus VAT and product costs.

Retainer – a set fee you pay a company or person each month to fulfil a service for you.

Returns – items sent back to you by customers who no longer want them.

Reverse engineering – working backwards from a desired outcome, for example a specific profit margin, to identify how it could be achieved.

Royal Mail – UK postal service.

Sale or return (SOR) – the business buying the stock has the right to return any goods not sold for a credit.

Sales channels – the different places you sell your products. A physical shop, your own website and a craft market would be three different sales channels.

Sales data – the information you can download from your selling systems, ideally grouped by product.

Scarcity – a limited amount of an item. The demand is greater than the supply.

Season – the selling season assigned to a product. For example, in clothing there will be Spring/Summer and Autumn/Winter styles.

Seasonality – the season of a particular item.

Seasonless – a product that can be sold across seasons. For example, a basic white T-shirt or a necklace.

Selling fees – a percentage of sales taken by the payment provider and/or the sales channel you are selling through.

Selling price – the full retail price that an item is intended to be sold at.

SEO – search engine optimization. The process of making your website easily found by search engines and ranking higher in the search results.

Shop soiled – an item is damaged or gets dirty as a result of being on the shop floor.

Shopify – a software company that many e-commerce businesses use to build their own website.

Star – a best-selling product.

Stock – the amount of inventory that you currently own. It may take the form of finished products if you buy from other businesses or your own manufacturing, or it might be in the form of components if you make your own products.

Stock-keeping – the process of creating and maintaining accurate records of your stock.

Stock-keeping unit (SKU) – the unique identifier for a particular product used by retailers for analysis and inventory management. It is assigned at the lowest level of identification. For example, an SKU would refer to a "short-sleeve T-shirt in red, size 10".

Stock management system – software that allows you to track stock and sales.

Stock turn – how quickly you sell the stock that you buy.

Stockist – a shop or chain of shops that have bought your product at wholesale.

Style – a product, including all its variants. For example, "short-sleeve T-shirt".

Style/colour – one colour of a style. For example, "short-sleeve T-shirt in red".

Subcategory – a level below category. If "Cards" is a category, "Christmas cards" could be a subcategory.

Supplier – a business that you buy stock from.

Supplier manual – a document that almost all large retailers have that will help you when preparing and delivering their orders.

Tail – the stock in your business that only generates 20% of your sales. A key indicator of how healthy your business is.

Target cost price – the cost price that you need to achieve in order to hit your margin goal.

Templates – pre-made spreadsheets that you can fill in with your own details.

Test and learn – the process of purchasing small amounts of an item and then placing a repeat order if it sells well. A useful risk management technique.

Till point – also known as the cash desk, the place in the shop where you go to pay.

Topline – gross sales.

Trading – making decisions about your stock and promotional stance based on sales information.

Traffic – visitors to your website or store.

Trapped cash – stock that you own but are not selling.

Unique identifier – a number assigned to a particular product to make analysis easier.

Variant – the different options that one product has. Variants can include different colour or size options, for example.

VAT – Value Added Tax, a sales tax payable on goods and services.

VAT registration – the process of beginning to charge VAT on your products and services.

Vlookup – a formula that allows you to compare two different sets of data.

Wholesale – selling products in large quantities and at low prices, typically to be sold on by other retailers at a profit.

Worst seller – the most disappointing products in terms of overall sales but also how slowly they are selling compared to their stock.

WSSI – weekly sales and stock intake – a tool used by the majority of large retailers to manage their stock.

Zero sellers – products where you have sold zero during a specific time frame.

Zero-waste shop – shops that aim to eliminate packaging and encourage the use of containers from home to refill with items such as food and cleaning products.

INDEX

ACKNOWLEDGEMENTS

I'd like to thank all of my clients and club members, podcast listeners, social media followers, webinar attendees, challenge participants and email subscribers for the many, many questions you have asked me over the last four years. It's been absolutely invaluable in helping me shape what I wanted to say in this book.

There's nothing quite like spending hours live on video answering questions to help me translate my industry knowledge into something useful for small businesses. So many of you have been open and generous in sharing your thoughts, worries and challenges with me, thank you.

I could not have written this book without the support of my excellent Resilient Retail Club team. I am very grateful to Jo Harding, Kate Scott and Shairead Georgiou who kept everything running smoothly while I was preoccupied with writing.

Thank you to Alison Jones for her invaluable support as I took the book from proposal to reality, and for giving me the inspiration for the tiger metaphor in the first place. I am also grateful to the whole Practical Inspiration Publishing team for being such excellent professionals and answering all my questions. Thank you to Terka Acton and Lucy Werner who independently recommended Alison to me, which I took to be a good sign!

I have many wonderful business friends around me, including two business masterminds who make all the difference. Thank you to Annabel Gonifas, Caro Gomez, Chloe Slade, Emma Phipps, Joanne Griffin, Kate Evans, Laura Ludlow, Sasha Gupta and Therese Oertenblad for all your support and encouragement. I really appreciated how enthusiastic Fiona Minnett, Marienne Pachonick, Nicki

Capewell, Vicky Simmons and many others were when I shared my idea for the book!

Special thanks to Elizabeth Stiles for being a sounding board on a daily basis and to Martyna Borek for helping me keep calm and focused.

I am very grateful to Raz Widrich at @pedagogeeks for patiently spending many hours helping me comb through all of my material to arrange it in a more logical way. His help was invaluable with putting together the first outline for the book.

I was fortunate enough to have excellent beta readers who generously gave their time and input. Thank you to Ali Ribchester of TuttiFrutti Clothing (@tuttifrutticlothing), Carly Allison at We Are Pop (@wearepop), Fiona Fawcett at Plewsy (@helloplewsy), Jo McCarthy at Firain (@jo_at_ firain), my dear friend Luis Monteiro and Rosie Greener at Good Daze Jewellery (@gooddazejewellery) for all your helpful comments and insight.

The beautiful illustrations in the book are by Snigdha P who you can find on PeoplePerHour.com. She was a dream to work with and incredibly talented.

Thank you to my brother Richard Wilson for your encouragement and patience in answering questions about writing a non-fiction book, and to my mother Margot Wilson for both your practical support and your belief in my ability to achieve what I set out to do. To all my family and friends, thank you for patiently listening while I explained how tigers related to product businesses!

I am *not* grateful to my cat, Neptune, who spared no opportunity to stand on my keyboard while I was writing and shredded several pages of the manuscript in an attempt to prove that tiger spirits are not so easily tamed.

My greatest thanks, of course, belongs to Carl for being my biggest cheerleader and to Cameron and Frances for simply being the best.

ABOUT THE AUTHOR

Catherine Erdly is an award-winning small business retail expert, podcast host, speaker and writer, recently named one of the top 100 retail influencers in the world by Rethink Retail. She has over two decades' experience in the retail industry, including 17 years managing budgets up to £400 million for some of the largest names in the high street in the UK and USA.

More recently, she has worked with hundreds of small and start-up independent businesses and brands to grow their sales, manage their stock and improve their business resilience through one-to-one consultancy and her membership group, The Resilient Retail Club.

Catherine is a Forbes.com contributor on the subject of starting and scaling a product business, a judge for the Good Retail Awards, on the editorial board of *Modern Retail*, a Small Business Britain champion and was awarded the UK's top sales adviser in 2021 by Enterprise Nation. She has been featured on national radio, television and press to give her insight into retail news and industry trends and hosts the popular The Resilient Retail Game Plan podcast.